MW01284928

30

MAP GUIDE TO
GERMAN PARISH REGISTERS

Kingdom of Saxony II
Kreishauptmannschäfter
Bautzen, Chemnitz and Dresden
with full index of included towns

by Kevan M. Hansen

© Kevan M. Hansen, 2009

Family Roots Publishing Company
PO Box 830
Bountiful, Utah 84011
www.FamilyRootsPublishing.com

Printed in the United States of America

13 12 11 10 09   5 4 3 2 1

Volume 26 – Soft Cover (FR0051)
ISBN-13: 978-1-933194-43-1   ISBN-10: 1-933194-43-X

Volume 26 – Hard Cover (FR0052)
ISBN-13: 978-1-933194-44-8   ISBN-10: 1-933194-44-8

Library of Congress Control Number: 2007939546

Volume 26 of the Map Guide to German Parish Registers series

Softbound edition front cover photography courtesy of James A. Derheim, European Focus, Inc.

This photograph is of a church in Moravia (Czech Republic) and is typical of those churches found throughout Europe

FOREWORD

This book, *Map Guide to German Parish Registers - Kingdom of Saxony II,* is part of a series compiled to make accessing German records easier. Its purpose is to aid in identifying what church records to search if a specific town is known. If only a general area is known, perhaps from a passenger list or naturalization record, this resource can also aid in identifying which church parishes can be found in that locality and facilitate accessing those records. Lastly, this resource can empower the researcher when confronted with the necessity of a radius search. Previously such searches required spending extensive time with a gazetteer and map, when available, in order to identify possible surrounding parishes. The graphical view portrayed in the accompanying maps makes identifying neighboring parishes, or perhaps districts, a task of minutes rather than hours. By referring to the included microfilm numbers for the Family History Library it can quickly be determined if records are available to search locally or if correspondence is required.

This compilation is *not meant* to serve as a beginner's guide to conducting German research. Numerous books are available instructing how to conduct German genealogical research. However, due to the individual history of the kingdoms, duchies, electorates, and principalities that comprised historical Germany, many resources are unique to a given area. Included with the parish maps is a listing of resources specific to the Kingdom of Saxony. These include records that have been microfilmed and are available at the Family History Library as well as resources that must be obtained in Germany. It is my hope that this resource can help alleviate the trepidation some people have about conducting German genealogical research. By streamlining this part of the research process you can spend your time obtaining more records of your ancestors and adding to your own personal history.

Kevan M. Hansen, 2009
kevan.hansen@gmail.com

TABLE OF CONTENTS

Part I

Kreishauptmannschaft Leipzig
      Amtshauptmannschaft Borna
      Amtshauptmannschaft Döbeln
      Amtshauptmannschaft Grimma
      Amtshauptmannschaft Leipzig
      Amtshauptmannschaft Oschatz
      Amtshauptmannschaft Rochlitz
Kreishauptmannschaft Zwickau
      Amtshauptmannschaft Auerbach
      Amtshauptmannschaft Oelsnitz
      Amtshauptmannschaft Plauen
      Amtshauptmannschaft Schwarzenberg
      Amtshauptmannschaft Zwickau

INTRODUCTION

A major genealogical brick wall for most Americans is the transition across the ocean to the ancestral homeland in Europe. Locating where the immigrant ancestor was born, and lived prior to emigration, challenges Americans; not because it can't be done, but because the research is often unique, the language is foreign, and sometimes the names have changed.

In United States research, connecting family ties from one generation to another can often be rapidly accomplished – using census records, vital records, probates, military records, obituaries, and so forth. On many occasions, I've extended American families back four or five generations, all in one afternoon of research.

In Germany, with the exception of Mecklenburg Schwerin, few censuses exist, and most family research is accomplished by the use of local parish registers. While early nineteenth-century civil birth registrations exist for some areas, principally those invaded by Napolean, civil registration should not be counted on for the majority of Germanic vital record research.

For Americans, finding the place in Germany usually requires first locating some clue found in America that spells out the town where the ancestor lived in Germany.

Searching in Baden, Wuerttemberg, Hessen, Bavaria, etc. is totally hopeless unless the name is extremely rare. In that case, and assuming relatives remained in the area, it may be possible to locate where the family lived by using directory information available online today. The most popular site used currently is the Geogen Surname Mapping site, found at: http://christoph.stoepel. net/geogen/en/Default.aspx. If this route is taken, then additional records found in Germany and/or America are usually essential in order for the researcher to know for certain that they have located the correct ancestral family. This might include family sources found with cousins in Germany. An ancestral family in the old country may be identified by locating a similar family in immigration and census records found in America. However, finding some clue in records found in America is nearly always necessary.

Also keep in mind the fact that the family name could have been spelled differently than it is today. Not that it was "changed at Ellis Island," but it may have been Americanized upon the immigration of your ancestor. It might also be found in the records in a phonetic form that does not match the typical spelling, or it could have been mis-transcribed by indexers of today's databases and indexes.

It is essential for American genealogists to first locate artifacts with the American family. This usually means that we must broaden the concept of family to include aunts, uncles, and cousins, no matter how far removed they are in the bloodline. To insure success, locate all the descendents of the immigrant ancestor. Living descendents could have letters, photographs, or naturalization papers. In genealogy "all family members are created equal." It is just as important to research the descendents of the siblings of your ancestors as it is to research the ancestors themselves. It will often be one of these cousins that holds the clue needed to ascertain the birthplace of your ancestor.

Records that might result in finding the hometown in the old country include newspapers (ethnic included), church records, immigrant aid society records, military pension files, homestead records, passport applications, and county histories. As an example, I first found the birthplace of my immigrant ancestor, Charles Meitzler, by locating a family sketch, printed in *Landmarks of Monroe County*, published in 1895. The sketch said "Mr. Meitzler was born at Kriegsfeld, Rhinepfalz, Germany, the son of a well to do farmer." It doesn't get much better than that.

Immigration records are much easier to research today than they were just a few years ago. Passenger lists can be located online at Ancestry.com, EllisIsland.org, and CastleGarden.org. The Hamburg Passenger Lists (giving the last residence of the emigrant) covering the years 1850 through 1934 are now available at Ancestry.de. Digitized passenger lists found at Ancestry.com start in 1820, and cover most of the major American seaports. Keep in mind that prior to 1892, there are very few passenger lists that give the immigrant's place of birth, since United States laws did not require it. For this reason, don't count on finding your ancestor's hometown in the passenger lists. However, since indexes are now available at the above-mentioned websites, these resources can typically be searched with reasonable success. Just don't expect to be researching German records immediately based on what you find in the passenger lists.

The same goes for naturalization records. Found in almost any court where your ancestor resided, these records can be interesting, but often not all that helpful. Between 1828 and 1906, the U.S. government only required that the court record the name of the alien, date of court appearance, the country to which allegiance is being dropped, and names of any witnesses. More information may be found, including birthplace or port of embarkation, but don't count on it. Note that the year of immigration, as well as naturalization status can be found in the 1900, 1910, 1920, and 1930 censuses. The 1920 census also includes the year of naturalization.

Researching neighbors and associates is often the ticket to locating where your ancestor came from. If you can't find documents that specifically give that data for your ancestor, try locating the information for those who they may have traveled with, went to church with, or who lived nearby. Our ancestors didn't often emigrate alone (although it was possible). Immigrants often joined family or friends who already lived in America. The opposite may have also taken place. Friends and relatives who left records that may still be extant today might have joined them in America. Don't overlook this important research technique.

The *Map Guide to German Parish Registers* series revolutionizes the locating of German immigrant ancestors, by allowing the researcher to quickly determine where their ancestor went to church, based upon where they lived. Although this information can be found in the text and footnotes of various Germanic gazetteers, they are often difficult to read and not readily available.

This series transforms this aspect of German research, making the parish, and therefore the records, faster and much easier to find.

First, using the techniques mentioned above, locate the name of the town where your ancestor was born. Second, find that town in the appropriate *Map Guide* index and turn to the Lutheran or Catholic Town Key. Next, let the town number direct you to the target parish in the Parish Key. The target parish should be the place where your ancestor went to church. Using the number assigned to the parish, check out the map on the opposite page. This map shows you the relationship of the parishes to each other. Having the information in map form allows the researcher to do a radius search of the surrounding parishes. It's important to do radius searches of nearby parishes, where you can often find evidence of extended family, and occasionally records of your own ancestor, who may have been more comfortable there than in their home parish. Keeping in mind that the clues gathered in America may not have led to the birthplace, but a nearby town, radius searches become even more important. When it is necessary to do a radius search, the *Map Guides* become increasingly more valuable.

Many German parish registers have been microfilmed and are available through the Family History Library and its Family History Centers. If this is the case, the initial film number for that parish is also found in the Parish Key, thus speeding your research.

German research is challenging for Americans, but by no means impossible. Using these volumes and the techniques found in the preceding text, you should have a good chance of success.

Leland K. Meitzler - 2009

HISTORICAL BACKGROUND

The area that became known as Saxony derived its name from the Saxons, one of the many tribal confederations which arose throughout Germany. The Saxons themselves were named after the *Sax*, a stone knife, in common use by the tribe. Originally settled on the North Sea, this tribal confederation conquered lands to the West in the third and fourth centuries. Their holdings eventually expanded to include most of Northern Germany. The western border of their lands extended almost to the Rhine River with only a small portion along the river itself remaining under the control of the Franks.

With the exception of the Saxons, the remaining Germanic tribes were united under the leadership of Clovis I, who ruled from 481-511. Clovis, along with the population of this new Frankish kingdom, accepted Christianity. The refusal of the Saxons to be governed by the Franks led to open conflict over the next century. Many of the Christian missionaries sent to convert the Saxons were killed or at the least, driven from their lands. It was not until Charlemagne rose to power among the Franks that the Saxons were finally conquered. The wars leading to this conquest are often known as the "religious wars" and lasted over three decades from 771-804. The conversion of the Saxons was overseen by St. Sturmi who died in 779. Following his death the Saxon lands were divided into missionary districts and eventually organized into dioceses. Charlemagne and his followers founded many of the monasteries throughout the area.

After the death of Charlemagne's son, Louis "the Pious," in 840, conflict arose between his heirs regarding the many territories which had been under his control. The Treaty of Verdun, signed in 843, divided the many lands between Louis' three sons; Lothair I, Charles "the Bald," and Louis "the German." The lands east of the Rhine and north and east of Italy, which included the lands of the Saxons, were known as the East Frankish Kingdom. It was from this area that Germany developed through gain and loss of lands through the centuries.

Due to weak or ineffective kings, each of the Germanic tribes was forced to rely on itself for protection and local rule. This was particulary true of those tribes in the North that fought the onslaught of the Norsemen and those in the East who continually held back the encroachment of the Slavs. The medieval duchy of Saxony was established with the first Saxon duke, Otto I der Erlauchte, "the Illustrious." His son, Heinrich I der Vogelsteller, "the Fowler," was crowned the first King of Germany, which he ruled from 918-936. The German influence was expanded under the rule of Henry's son, Otto II der Grosse, "the Great," who was crowned Holy Roman Emperor by the pope.

Otto II acquired many Slavonic holdings during his reign and saw that Christianity was established within them. He divided the duchy into margraviates, which aided in political as well as ecclesiastical control of each area. Much of the land controlled by the dukes of Saxony at this time was divided and lost over the years. An example would be Nordmark, or Northern Mark, which later was given to Prussia as part of the province of Sachsen. The central area, and what is associated with the Kingdom of Saxony was known as Mark Meissen, or the Margraviate of Meissen.

In 936, Otto II appointed Count Hermann, son of Billung von Stubenskorn, as Margrave of Saxony. During Otto's absences Hermann was left as military leader with much of the authority of the German duke. Although never officially named in historical records as duke, his position of trust and power have led him to be named the first Duke of Saxony. His son, Bernard I, was officially given the ducal title which remained as an inheritable right in the Billung line. The electorate continued in the Billung line down to Magnus who died in 1106.

At that time the Billung line became extinct and the duchy was given to Lothair von Süpplinberg who became King of Germany in 1125 and later Holy Roman Emperor. Upon his death the control of the duchy was transferred to Heinrich II Jasmirgott, "the Proud," of the Guelph family. When his son, Heinrich III der Löwe, "the Lion," gained control of the duchy he expanded German control further north but his decision to refuse to aid Frederick I Barbarossa in Lombardy led to an immense reduction to Saxony's holdings. The ban placed by Frederick I led to dividing up of Saxon lands at the Diet of Gelnhausen in 1181.

The western lands were divided and known as Westphalia. Saxony itself was further divided into smaller districts which saw control exercised over them by the bishops of the area. The districts in Lower Saxony were comprised of the lands of Hannover, the northern province of Saxony, and the city of Hamburg. The districts in Upper Saxony were made up of the Kingdom of Saxony and the many duchies, principalities, etc. which comprised Thuringen.

In 1356 Emperor Charles IV issued *die Goldene Bull*, or Golden Bull, a change in the law of electing the emperor. It decreed that seven electors would decide the Roman King who would then, in most cases, be crowned emperor by the pope. This elevated the Duchy of Saxony to the status of an electorate that was given to the Duchy of Wittenberg. The electorate itself was passed down through the system of primogeniture ensuring that the oldest heir remained in control and the lands themselves were not divided over and over among many successive heirs.

The heirs in this line became extinct in 1422 and the Saxon lands and electorate were given to Frederick I der Streitbare, "the Warlike," who was the Margrave of Meissen and a descendant of Otto I. These lands remained under control of one family until Frederick I's son, Frederick II der Sanftmütige, "the Gentle," died in 1464. Although initially ruled jointly, these territories were divided in 1485 into two branches of the family which are known as the Albertine line, led by Albrecht der Behertze, "the Bold," and the Ernestine line, led by his brother Ernest. Albrecht, or Albert, received the Thuringian lands and the electorate. His brother Ernest received the Margraviate of Meissen. These were designated as the Electorate of Saxony and the Duchy of Saxony.

In the ensuing years the Electorate of Saxony became the focal point for the Reformation throughout Germany. The elector, Friederick III der Weise, "the Wise," became known for enlightenment and devotion to religion. By the early sixteenth century his personal chapel reportedly held 17, 443 holy relics of the church. The institution for which he is perhaps best known was the foundation of the University of Wittenberg in 1502. By 1508 the monk, Martin Luther, was found as a teacher of philosophy there and one of the preachers at the castle chapel. A decade later, following Luther's posting of his ninety-five theses at the Wittenberg church, Friederick III intervened and provided protection for Martin Luther. In 1521 Friedrick III saw that an agreement was reached with Charles V for Luther's safe conduct to and from the Diet of Worms. When the Edict of Worms was issued providing a complete ban on following, supporting, or defending Martin Luther, as well as his apprehension as a heretic, Friederick III again intervened with a fake attack against Luther's party on the way back to Wittenberg. He was subsequently hidden at Wartburg Castle overlooking the city of Eisenach.

The influence of the Reformation spread throughout the electorate. This effort led to the confiscation of church lands, deposing of any remaining Catholic priests, and the desire to drive all Catholic influence from their lands. Johann der Beständige, "the Constant," was a member of the Smalkaldic League, the alliance formed of Lutheran princes to defend themselves against Charles V. Johann Friederick der Grossmütige, "the Magnanimous," was the son of Johann der Beständige and also one of the leaders of the Smalkaldic League. After leading attacks against the diocese of Meissen and Naumburg-Zeitz, among others, he was captured on April 24, 1547 by Charles V at the Battle of Mühlberg an der Elbe. The following May he was forced to yield the electorate to Moritz (or Maurice) of Meissen, leaving only the Thuringen lands under his control. The subsequent history for this branch of the family can be followed further in *Map Guide to German Parish Registers, Thuringia.*

The leaders of Margrave of Meissen had, until shortly before this time been staunch supporters of the Catholic cause. This changed under the rule of Heinrich IV der Fromme, "the Pious," who was influenced by his wife, Katharina von Mecklenburg, who was sympathetic to the Lutheran cause. Conflict between the Catholics and Protestants remained a large part of the Saxon history down through the Thirty Years War (1618 - 1648) which, as with many areas of Germany, saw great destruction through the region. Many German states lost between fifteen and thirty percent of their population during this conflict with some, such as Württemberg, losing as much as three-fourths of its population.

Following the Thirty Years War the leadership of Saxony remained Lutheran, along with its population. When Friedrich August II der Fette, "the Fat," inherited control of the electorate the Saxon leadership were once again Catholic. In spite of this, the population of Saxony remained staunchly Lutheran.

In 1806, during Prussia's war with Napolean, Saxony backed neither side. When Napolean declared that it would be treated as a hostile nation if it did not back him, Saxony united with France and became a member of the Confederation of the Rhine. At the Congress of Vienna, Saxony lost most of its holdings. Most of this was given to Prussia including the former Saxe-Wittenberg. Those lands were formed into the Province of Sachsen. Saxony was elevated to the status of a kingdom but its lands had been reduced to slightly over forty percent of its holdings prior to the Congress of Vienna.

In 1815 Saxony sided with Austria in the Austro-Prussian War. Upon Austria's defeat, Saxony might have fully lost its lands to Prussia had the Austrian Emperor not interceded on its behalf. It was however forced to join the North German Confederation headed by Prussia. In 1871 Saxony joined the German Empire. Saxony was a member of the Weimar Republic in 1918 and following World War II it was given to the Soviet Union as part of the settlement of the Potsdam Conference. In 1949 when the German Democratic Republic, or East Germany, was established it became part of those lands. It was reunified with the remainder of Germany in 1990 and is currently part of the Free State of Saxony which includes some areas that had formerly belonged to Silesea.

On December 1, 1880 Bavaria had a population of 2,9728,65 with 97% of its population Lutheran, 2.5% Lutheran and the remainder Jewish and other religions.

RULERS OF SAXONY

Note: The charts below detail only the main rulers and do not show cadet branches of the family, each of which had their own rulers.

Dukes of Saxony

d. aft 531	Hadugato
d. aft 627	Berthoald
d. aft 743	Theoderic
d. 7 Jan 810	Widukind
d. aft 811	Abo
d. abt 840	Banzleib
abt 850	Liudolf
d. bef 880	Bruno
880 - 912	Otto I der Erlauchte, "the Illustrious."
918 - 936	Henry I der Vogelsteller, "the Fowler," King of Saxony.
936 - 962	Otto II der Grosse, "the Great," King of Saxony, and later Holy Roman Emperor (962-973).
961 - 973	Herman Billung, Duke of Saxony.
973 - 1011	Bernard I, Duke of Saxony.
1011 - 1059	Bernard II, Duke of Saxony.
1059 - 1072	Ordulf, Duke of Saxony.
1072 - 1106	Magnus, Duke of Saxony.
1106 - 1137	Lothair von Süpplinberg, Duke of Saxony, later King of Germany (1125-1137), and Holy Roman Emperor 1133-1137).
1137 - 1139	Heinrich II, Jasmirgott, "the Proud." He also held the title Duke of Bavaria.
1139 - 1142	Albrecht der Bär, "the Bear." He was also the first Margrave of Brandenburg.
1142 - 1180	Heinrich III der Löwe, "the Lion." He also held the title Duke of Bavaria.
1180 - 1212	Bernard III, Duke of Saxony.
1212 - 1260	Albrecht II, Duke of Saxony, and Margrave of Brandenburg.
1260 - 1286	Johann I, Duke of Saxony, joint ruler with his brother Albrecht III.
1260 - 1298	Albrecht III, Duke of Saxony, joint ruler with his brother, Johann I.
1464 - 1500	Albrecht der Behertze, "the Bold."
1500 - 1539	George der Bärtige, "the Bearded."
1539 - 1541	Heinrich IV der Fromme, "the Pious."
1541 - 1547	Moritz, became Elector in 1547.

Dukes of Saxe-Lauenburg

1272 - 1285	Johann I, Duke of Saxe-Lauenburg, and former Duke of Saxony.
1285 - 1305	Johann II, Duke of Saxe-Lauenburg.
1296 - 1305	Albrecht III, Duke of Saxe-Lauenburg.
1296 - 1305	Erich I, Duke of Saxe-Lauenburg.
1401 - 1412	Erich IV, Duke of Saxe-Lauenburg, and formerly Duke of Saxe-Ratzeburg.
1412 - 1436	Erich V, Duke of Saxe-Lauenburg.
1412 - 1436	Johann IV, Duke of Saxe-Lauenburg.
1436 - 1463	Bernhard III, Duke of Saxe-Lauenburg.
1463 - 1507	Johann V, Duke of Saxe-Lauenburg.
1507 - 1543	Magnus I, Duke of Saxe-Lauenburg.
1543 - 1581	Franz I, Duke of Saxe-Lauenburg.
1581 - 1603	Magnus II, Duke of Saxe-Lauenburg.
1603 - 1619	Franz II, Duke of Saxe-Lauenburg.
1619 - 1656	August, Duke of Saxe-Lauenburg.
1656 - 1665	Julius Heinrich, Duke of Saxe-Lauenburg.
1665 - 1666	Franz Erdmann, Duke of Saxe-Lauenburg.
1666 - 1689	Julius Franz, Duke of Saxe-Lauenburg.

Dukes of Saxe-Mölln-Bergdorf

1305 - 1321	Johann II, Duke of Saxe-Mölln Bergdorf, and formerly Duke of Saxe-Lauenburg.
1321 - 1343	Albrecht IV, Duke of Saxe-Mölln Bergdorf.
1343 - 1356	Johann III, Duke of Saxe-Mölln Bergdorf.
1356 - 1370	Albrecht V, Duke of Saxe-Mölln Bergdorf.
1370 - 1401	Erich III, Duke of Saxe-Mölln Bergdorf.

Dukes of Saxe-Ratzeburg

1305 - 1308	Albrecht III, Duke of Saxe-Ratzeburg, and formerly Duke of Saxe-Lauenburg.
1305 - 1361	Erich I, Duke of Saxe-Ratzeburg.
1361 - 1368	Erich II, Duke of Saxe-Ratzeburg.
1368 - 1401	Erich IV, Duke of Saxe-Ratzeburg.

Electors of Saxony

1356 - 1370	Rudolf II, formerly Duke of Saxe-Wittenberg.
1370 - 1388	Wenzel / Wenceslaus
1388 - 1419	Rudolf III
1419 - 1422	Albert III

1423 - 1428	Frederick I der Streitbare, "the Warlike," Margraveof Meissen.
1428 - 1464	Frederick II der Sanftmütige, "the Gentle," Margrave of Meissen. and Landgrave of Thuringia.
1428 - 1445	William III
1464 - 1485	Ernest
1464 - 1485	Albert der Behertze, "the Bold."
1486 - 1525	Friederick III der Weise, "the Wise."
1525 - 1532	Johann der Beständige, "the Constant."
1532 - 1547	Johann Friederick der Grossmütige, "the Magnanimous."
1547 - 1553	Moritz
1553 - 1586	August I
1586 - 1591	Christian I
1591 - 1611	Christian II
1611 - 1656	Johann Georg I
1656 - 1680	Johann Georg II
1680 - 1691	Johann Georg III
1691 - 1694	Johann Georg IV
1694 - 1733	Friedrich August der Starke, "the Strong."
1733 - 1763	Friedrich August der Fette, "the Fat."
1763	Friedrich Christian
1763 - 1806	Friedrich August III der Gerechte, "the Just."

Kings of Saxony

1806 - 1827	Friedrich August III der Gerechte, "the Just," formerly Elector of Saxony.
1827 - 1836	Anton der Gütige, "the Benevolent."
1836 - 1854	Friedrich August II
1854 - 1873	Johann
1873 - 1892	Albert der Gute, "the Good."
1902 - 1904	Georg
1904 - 1918	Friedrich August III

SAXONY GENEALOGICAL RESOURCES

CIVIL REGISTRATION

Civil registration in Saxony began on January 1, 1876. Birth, death, and marriage records were filed at the *standesamt* or local civil registration office. The office for towns throughout Germany can be identified in *Meyers Lexikon*:

> *Meyers Orts- und Verkehrs-Lexikon des Deutschen Reichs*, E. Utrecht and
> Raymond S. Wright, (Baltimore: Genealogical Publishing Co., Inc., 2000 reprint
> of Leipzig: Bibliographisches Institute, 1912-13) FHL 943 E5mo 2000 v.1-3.

In many areas civil records were kept much earlier but kept inconsistently by local authorities. Marriage contracts and other civil agreements can be found in the local *standesamt*. If microfilmed, and available at the Family History Library, such records would be cataloged under the local jurisdiction often with a cross-reference for each town.

EMIGRATION

Records filed by residents leaving Germany are available in each regional emigration office or *auswanderungsamt*. The Family History Library has not filmed all of these records making it necessary to obtain them from the individual offices. When unavailable these must be obtained from the regional archive offices for each district. In addition, secondary collections have been published which provide detailed information about those leaving the area:

Auswanderungspässe, 1837-1839, 1876 - 1927 [Permission to emigrate requests of Hohenstein-Ernstthal, Sachsen, Germany], (manuscript in Stadtarchiv Ernstthal) FHL films #2420583 and #2420579.

Auswanderungs-, Heimatscheine, etc. 1835-1864 [Emigration, origin certificates for Treuen, Sachsen, Germany], (manuscript in Kreisarchiv Auerbach) FHL film #1475367.

Heimatsangelegenheiten, Ausländerausweisung, Ehen im Ausland, etc. 1835-1937, [Documentations of origin for Werdau (AH Zwickau), Sachsen, Germany] (manuscript in Stadt and Kreisarchiv Zwickau) FHL film #1476170.

Wanderbücher 1769-1873 [Removal permissions of Zwickau, Sachsen, Germany], (manuscript in Stadtarchiv Zwickau) FHL film #1340804.

Wanderbücher, 1765-1868 [Migration registration of residents of Chemnitz, Sachsen, Germany], (manuscript in Stadtarchiv Weimar) FHL film #1346513.

Auswanderungen, Entlassungen, Heimatscheine 1841-1921 [Emigrants, releases, origin certificates for Annaberg, Sachsen, Germany], (manuscript in Kreisarchiv Annaberg) FHL film #1475324.

Dresdener Auswanderer nach Übersee 1850-1903, Karl Werner Klüber (Mitteldeutsche Familienkunde - Bd. 3, Jahrg. 11-13, Heft 3 (1970-Juli/Sept. 1972) FHL 943 B2mf v. 3.

LINEAGE BOOKS

The town lineage book, known as an *ortsippenbuch or dorfsippenbuch*, can be found for many regions of Germany. Compiled from the earliest parish and town records, these published sources usually show data arranged by family units, and organized by surname. Entries for each family may include birth or christening dates, marriage dates, and burial or death dates for each member of the family. Branches of the family that have moved away often contain cross-references to other lineage books or references to emigration to the United States or other foreign countries. Town lineages detailed in periodicals can be identified in the following bibliographies:

Bibliographie der Ortsippenbücher in Deutschland, Franz Heinzmann (Düsseldorf: Heinzmann, 1991) FHL 943 D23h, or film #678491.

The list below shows towns that either have lineage books of their own or that have been published for them, or they are included as part of the larger church parish jurisdiction. The call number follows each entry if a copy is available at the Family History Library.

Annaberger Familien des 16. Jahrhunderts, Wolfgang Lorenz (Annaberg-Buchholz: Adam-Ries-Bund, 1997) FHL 943.21 D2a.

Familienbuch für Schwarzbach/Krs. Annaberg, 1540-1838, Waldus Nestler und Elke Kretzschmar (Leipzig: Volkmar Weiss, 1993) FHL 943 B4sd and film #1183629.

Familienbuch für die Kirchgemeinde Arnsfeld mit Grumbach, Satzung und Steinbach 1574-1693, Renate Hannemann und Wilfried Gerbig (Leipzig: Volkmar Weiss, 1995) FHL 943.21/A1 D2h.

Dorf-Sippenbuch Leutewitz, Verein für bäuerliche Sippenkunde und bäuerliches Wappenwesen (Goslar: Blut und Boden Verlag, 1938) FHL 943.21/L1 D2v and film #1045364.

Genealogische Tabellen über Zittauer Familien, Karl Fritz Engelmann (microfilm of manuscript in Zentrallstelle fü Genealogie) [Register of the families of Zittau covering 17th-19th centuries. Volumes 10-11 include surrounding towns of Chemnitz, Grossschönau, Oderwitz, Herwigsdorf, Görlitz, Lindau, Bautzen, and Bernstadt.] FHL film #1866009.

Familienbuch des Kirchspiels Waldkirchen mit Grünhainichen und Börnichen: 1548 bis 1715, Gisele Lorenz (Kleve: Arbeitsgemeinschaft für mitteldeutsche Familienforschung, 1999) FHL 943.22/W5 D2L.

PERIODICALS AND GENEALOGICAL COLLECTIONS

Germany as a whole has numerous periodicals that are currently or have previously been published. Because they are not limited to a specific region, it is possible to find records and family histories, regardless of the region in which a family lived. Two key indexes are available to aid in accessing these many publications:

Der Schlüssel: Gesamtinhaltsverzeichnisse für genealogische, heraldische und historische Zeitschriftenreihen mit Orts-, Sach-, und Namenregistern, 9 vols. (Göttingen: Heinz Reise Verlag, 1950-1986) FHL 943 D25sc.

Familiengeschichtliche Quellen: Zeitschrift familiengeschichtlicher Quellennachweise, 17 vols. (Neustadt/Aisch: Degener, 1926) FHL 943 B2fq, film #496680, fiche #6000817.

In addition to periodicals, numerous genealogical collections are available for Germany. Two collections that include biographies, histories, lineages, and family data are as follows:

Führende Persönichkeiten, Institut zur Erforschung Historischer Führungsgeschichten Bensheim (SLC, Utah: Genealogical Society of Utah, 1980-1983) FHL film #0092838.

Deutches Geschlechterbuch (German lineage book), 194 + volumes (Limburg a/d Lahn: C.A. Starke, 1889-) FHL 943 D2dg, film #491876. An index to the first 150 volumes is found in *Stammfolgen-Verzeichnisse für das genealogische Handbuch des Adels und das deutsche Geshlechterbuch* (Limburg a/d Lahn, C.A. Starke, 1969) FHL 943 D2dg, film #1183565, fiche #6053506.

ARCHIVES AND REPOSITORIES

Regional and State Archives

Sächsisches Staatsarchiv
Wilhelm-Buck-Str. 4
01097 Dresden
Fax: 0351/5643739
E-mail: poststelle@sta.smi.sachsen.de
Website: http://www.staatsarchiv.smi.sachsen.de

Sächsisches Hauptstaatsarchiv Dresden
Aussenstelle Bautzen
Seidauer Strasse 2
02625 Bautzen

Sächsisches Hauptstaatsarchiv Dresden
Aussenstelle Chemnitz
Technik Center Chemnitz

Sächsisches Hauptstaatsarchiv Dresden
Aussenstelle Freiberg / Bergarchiv
Kirchgasse 11
09599 Freiberg

Sächsisches Hauptstaatsarchiv Dresden
Aussenstelle Glauchau
Schloss Vorderglauchau
08371 Glauchau

Church Archives

Evangelisch-Lutherisches Landeskirchenamt Sachsens
Postfach 12 05 52
01006 Dresden
Fax: 490351/4692-109
E-Mail: kirche@evlks.de
Website: www.evlks.de

Regionalkirchenamt Chemnitz
Agricolastrasse 33
09112 Chemnitz
Fax: 0371 3810216
E-Mail: rka.chemnitz@evlks.de
(for the church districts of Aue, Auerbach, Annaberg, Chemnitz, Glauchau, Marienberg, Plauen und Zwickau)

Regionalkirchenamt Dresden
Kreuzstrasse 7
01067 Dresden
Fax: 0351 4923-348
E-Mail: rka.dresden@evlks.de
(for the church districts of Bautzen, Dresden Mitte, Dresden Nord, Freiberg, Grossenhain, Kamenz, Löbau-Zittau, Meissen and Pirna)

Evangelisch-Lutherisches Kirchenbezirk Annaberg
Evangelisch-Lutherisches Superintendentur Annaberg
Kleine Kirchgasse 23
09456 Annaberg-Buchholz
Fax: 03733 4269927
E-Mail: suptur.annaberg@evlks.de
Website: http://www.kirche-erzgebirge.de

Evangelisch-Lutherisches Kirchenbezirk Bautzen
Evangelisch-Lutherisches Superintendentur Bautzen
August-Bebel-Platz 11
02625 Bautzen
Fax: 03591 390934
E-Mail: suptur.bautzen@evlks.de
Website: http://www.kirchenbezirk-bautzen.de

Evangelisch-Lutherisches Kirchenbezirk Chemnitz
Evangelisch-Lutherisches Superintendentur Chemnitz
Theaterstrasse 25
09111 Chemnitz
Fax: 0371 4005624
E-Mail: suptur.chemnitz@evlks.de
Website: http://www.kirche-chemnitz.de

Evangelisch-Lutherisches Kirchenbezirk Dresden Mitte
Evangelisch-Lutherisches Superintendentur Dresden Mitte
An der Kreuzkirche 6
01067 Dresden
Fax: 0351 4393919
E-Mail: suptur.dresden_mitte@evlks.de
Website: http://www.elydia.de

Evangelisch-Lutherisches Kirchenbezirk Dresden Nord
Evangelisch-Lutherisches Superintendentur Dresden Nord
Martin-Luther-Platz 5
01099 Dresden
E-Mail: suptur.dresden_nord@evlks.de
Website: http://www.elydia.de

Evangelisch-Lutherisches Kirchenbezirk Freiberg
Evangelisch-Lutherisches Superintendentur Freiberg
Untermarkt 1
09599 Freiberg
Fax: 03731 300843
E-Mail: suptur.freiberg@evlks.de
Website: http://www.kirchenbezirk-freiberg.de

Evangelisch-Lutherisches Kirchenbezirk Glauchau
Evangelisch-Lutherisches Superintendentur Glauchau
Kirchplatz 7
08371 Glauchau
E-Mail: suptur.glauchau@evlks.de
Website: http://www.kirche-glauchau.de

Evangelisch-Lutherisches Kirchenbezirk Grossenhain
Evangelisch-Lutherisches Superintendentur Grossenhain
Naundorfer Strasse 29
01558 Grossenhain
Fax: 03522 502281
E-Mail: suptur.grossenhain@evlks.de
Website: http://www.kirchenbezirk-grossenhain.de

Evangelisch-Lutherisches Kirchenbezirk Kamenz
Evangelisch-Lutherisches Superintendentur Kamenz
Kirchstrasse 20
01917 Kamenz
Fax: (03578) 774816
E-Mail: Suptur.Kamenz@evlks.de

Evangelisch-Lutherisches Kirchenbezirk Löbau-Zittau
Evangelisch-Lutherisches Superintendentur Löbau-Zittau
Friedhofsstrasse 3
02708 Löbau
Fax: 03585 415773
E-Mail: suptur.loebau_zittau@evlks.de
Website: http://www.kirchenbezirk-loebau-zittau.de

Evangelisch-Lutherisches Kirchenbezirk Marienberg
Evangelisch-Lutherisches Superintendentur Marienberg
Dresdner Strasse 4
09557 Flöha
Fax: 03726 782564
E-Mail: suptur.marienberg@evlks.de

Evangelisch-Lutherisches Kirchenbezirk Meissen
Evangelisch-Lutherisches Superintendentur Meissen
Freiheit 9
01662 Meissen
Fax: 03521 451693
E-Mail: suptur.meissen@evlks.de
Website: http://www.kirchenbezirk-meissen.de

Evangelisch-Lutherisches Kirchenbezirk Pirna
Evangelisch-Lutherisches Superintendentur Pirna
Kirchplatz 13
01796 Pirna
Fax: (03501) 4612425
E-Mail: suptur.pirna@evlks.de
Website: http://www.kirchenbezirk-pirna.de

GAZETTEERS

August Schuhmann, *Vollständiges Staats-, Post-, und Zeitungs-Lexikon von Sachsen: enthaltend eine richtige und ausführliche geographische, topographische und historische Darstellung aller Städte, Flecken, Dörfer, Schlösser, Höfe, Gebirge, Wälder, Seen, Flüsse, etc., gesammter königl. und fürstl. sächsischer Lande, mit Einschluss des Fürstenthums Schwarzburg, des Erfurtschen Gebietes, so wie der Reussischen und Schönburgischen Besitzungen* (Hungen-Bellersheim: Familienarchiv Papsdorf, 2005) FHL film #824319.

Central Comité des statistischen Vereins für das Königreich Sachsen, *Neues alphabetisches Orts-Verzeichnis des Königreichs Sachsen nach der officiellen Nachrichten zusammengestellt*, [New alphabetical gazetteer for the Kingdom of Saxony] (Dresden: Walterschen Hofbuchhandlung, 1836).

Digitales Historisches Ortsverzeichnis von Sachsen
[Digital Historical Gazetteer of Saxony]
http://hov.isgv.de

HOW TO USE THIS BOOK

Each of the accompanying maps serves as a "snapshot" of the parishes in each district for the mid- to late-1800s. Unlike countries, such as Great Britain, whose parishes are precisely defined, German parishes are defined by what towns are assigned to each parish but without well defined boundaries. By working with digitized underlying maps of Germany, the parish boundaries were drawn to encompass those towns included in each individual parish. This provides a view of how the various parishes fit together and defines the boundaries of each district.

One should not suppose that all parishes have existed back into the fog of history. Instead, as one progresses backwards in research you may find that a given parish did not exist, for example, in the mid-1700s. By having a view of which parishes surround it, a researcher can begin to determine which parishes the town they are researching may have belonged to earlier. Likewise, an overview of how the parishes are arranged can facilitate a *radius search* of neighboring parishes. This search of neighboring parishes in an expanding circle, or *radius*, around the home parish can be more easily prioritized in order of parishes closest to furthest away.

This book is divided into four sections: one dealing with Saxony resources (page 207), two parts comprising maps of the administrative districts, with parish boundaries of the Lutheran (page 219) and Catholic (page 295), and one section showing record availablility for minority religions (page 361). Included in the back of the book is an index to all of the towns with page numbers for both Lutheran and Catholic sections.

The map section provides a graphical view of each district and its parishes, a parish key to the parishes themselves including the Family History Library microfilm numbers, and a listing of towns in that district. For example, the Lutheran map and town key for the *Amtshauptmannschaft*, or district, of Bautzen on pages 222 through 226 show that the town of Boblitz belonged to parish #12, which the parish key identifies as Bautzen parish. The parish key also shows microfilmed parish registers are available for the parish of Bautzen at the Family History Library on microfilm #1784307 and #1837513. Because microfilmed parish registers normally comprise more than one film, the number shown for a parish is the first microfilm in the series belonging to that register. By entering this number in the microfilm number search, in the Family History Library Catalog at www.family-search.org, a researcher can obtain a printout of all films for a given parish, and the years included on each one. If the parish registers have not been microfilmed, which is often the case, the researcher will be able, knowing the name of the parish their ancestors attended, to request records through correspondence. This will usually be to a district archive or the parish itself. Although maps are not provided for the minority religions, Family History Library microfilm numbers have been included when available.

If the specific town of residence of a given ancestor is known, the index at the back of the book can be consulted to determine which map to reference to locate records for that town. Numbering of parishes begins with #1 for each district on the Lutheran maps and continues on the Catholic maps until all parishes are numbered. This provides continuity in the maps and ensures that there is no overlap in the numbering between Lutheran and Catholic parishes in each district.

In order for a town to have been assigned to a particular parish there needed to be residents of that religious persuasion living in the town. In an area which was predominently one faith over another, many of the towns would not have had residents of the minority religion. As a result, the gazetteers do not provide an assigned parish for that town. Thus, if a town is referenced in *Map Guide to German Parish Registers, Kingdom of Saxony,* but there is no corresponding parish number assigned to it, the town was not specifically designated to attend a particular parish. This can be seen on the maps which may contain dozens of parishes for Lutheran or Catholic with one or two parishes for the opposite religion.

To determine the probable parish any residents would have attended when it has not been assigned, search the district listing for neighboring towns. The end result is that residents might have to travel long distances to attend church. The result is that many of the parishes having few citizens of that faith may comprise an entire district or even extend into neighboring districts.

Radius searching can be easily planned by referencing the map and town key to see which towns surround that of a given parish. Once identified, the microfilm numbers can be noted and the towns systematically examined.

Whenever a new town is identified in the original records it can be referenced against the index and town key to determine if it lies in the same parish, in a neighboring parish, or perhaps even a distant parish.

Overview of administrative districts,
Kreishauptmannschäfter, in the
Kingdom of Saxony

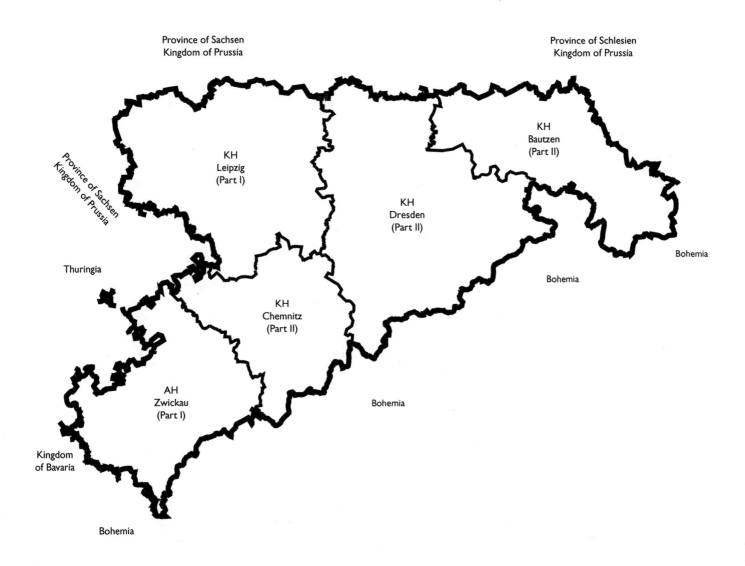

Province of Sachsen
Kingdom of Prussia

Province of Schlesien
Kingdom of Prussia

Province of Sachsen
Kingdom of Prussia

KH
Leipzig
(Part I)

KH
Bautzen
(Part II)

KH
Dresden
(Part II)

Thuringia

Bohemia

KH
Chemnitz
(Part II)

Bohemia

AH
Zwickau
(Part I)

Bohemia

Kingdom
of Bavaria

Bohemia

LUTHERAN PARISHES

Overview of districts, *Amtshauptmannschäfter*, in the
Kreishauptmannschaft Bautzen
Kingdom of Saxony - Part II

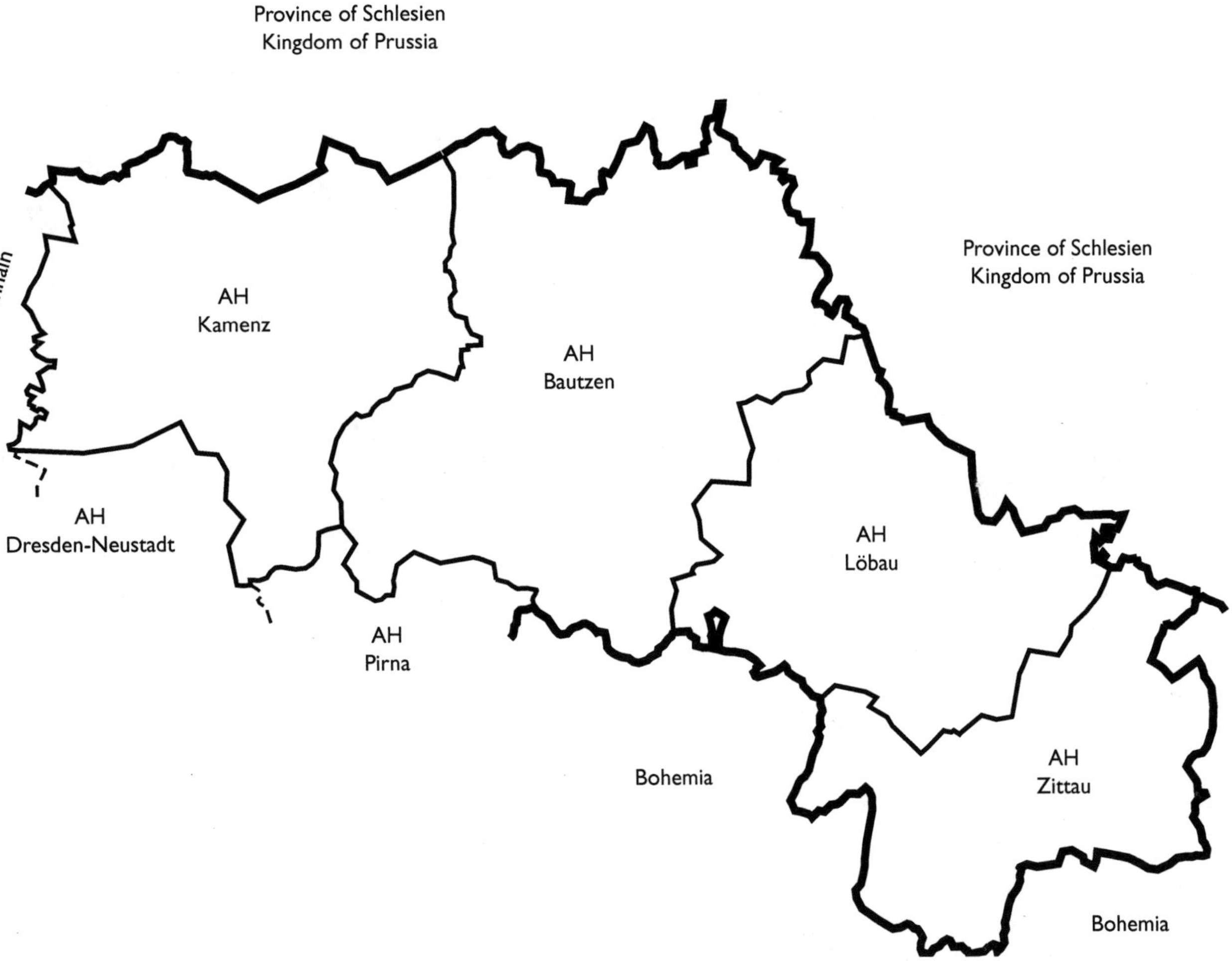

Province of Schlesien
Kingdom of Prussia

Province of Schlesien
Kingdom of Prussia

AH
Grossenhain

AH
Kamenz

AH
Bautzen

AH
Dresden-Neustadt

AH
Löbau

AH
Pirna

AH
Zittau

Bohemia

Bohemia

AMTSHAUPTMANNSCHAFT BAUTZEN
LUTHERAN PARISHES

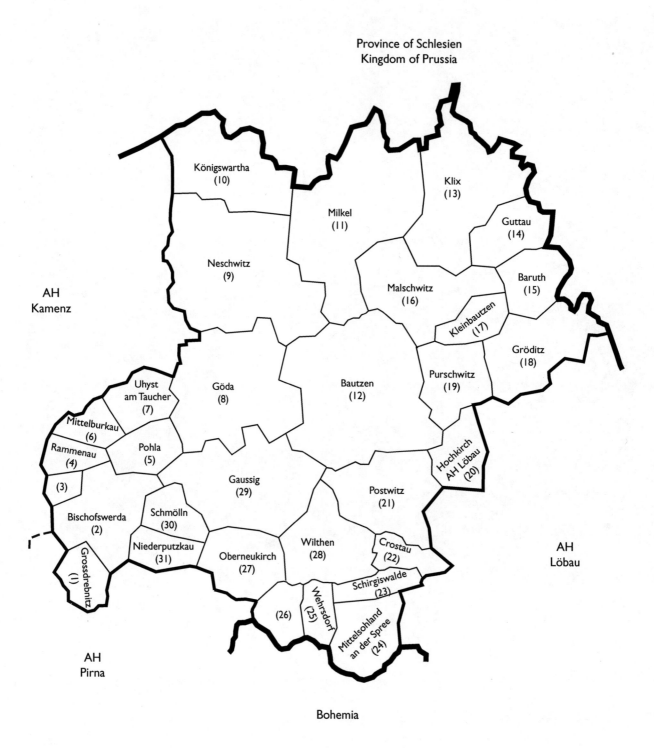

Province of Schlesien
Kingdom of Prussia

Königswartha
(10)

Klix
(13)

Milkel
(11)

Guttau
(14)

Neschwitz
(9)

Baruth
(15)

AH
Kamenz

Malschwitz
(16)

Kleinbautzen
(17)

Gröditz
(18)

Uhyst
am Taucher
(7)

Göda
(8)

Bautzen
(12)

Purschwitz
(19)

Mittelburkau
(6)

Pohla
(5)

Rammenau
(4)

Hochkirch
AH Löbau
(20)

(3)

Gaussig
(29)

Postwitz
(21)

Bischofswerda
(2)

Schmölln
(30)

AH
Löbau

Niederputzkau
(31)

Wilthen
(28)

Crostau
(22)

Grossdrebnitz
(1)

Oberneukirch
(27)

Schirgiswalde
(23)

Wehrsdorf
(25)

AH
Pirna

(26)

Mittelsohland
an der Spree
(24)

Bohemia

10 miles		20 miles	
10 km	20 km	30 km	

222

PARISH KEY

1. Grossdrebnitz.............	17. Kleinbautzen..............
2. Bischofswerda	18. Gröditz....................
3. Frankenthal	19. Purschwitz ....
4. Rammenau.................	20. Hochkirch
5. Pohla.......................	AH Löbau ....
6. Mittelburkau	21. Postwitz ....
7. Uhyst am Taucher.......	22. Crostau...................
8. Göda	23. Schirgiswalde ....
9. Neschwitz	24. Mittelsohland
10. Königswartha.............	an der Spree 1271408
11. Milkel	25. Wehrsdorf.................
12. Bautzen..................... 1784307	26. Stenigtwolmsdorf ....
.... 1837513	27. Oberneukirch ....
13. Klix........................	28. Wilthen ....
14. Guttau	29. Gaussig 1196226
15. Baruth	30. Schmölln..................
16. Malschwitz	31. Niederputzkau.............

TOWN KEY

Alberts-Rachlau 20	Boblitz............................12	Cannewitz.......................8
Alberts-Rackel 20	Bocka bei Luppa..............11	Cannewitz bei Gröditz 18
Altscheidenbach 24	Bolbritz...........................8	Carlsberg 22
Arnsdorf........................29	Bornitz 11	Carlsdorf........................8
Auritz 12	Brehmen.........................13	Carlsdorf........................11
Äusserst Sohland 24	Breske 8	Carlsruhe 24
Barosche 13	Brettnig..........................3	Casslau..........................9
Baruth...........................15	Briesing.........................16	Coblenz 8
Basankwitz 12	Briessnitz.......................18	Cölln 12
Baschütz........................19	Brohna...........................11	Commerau bei Kauppa....13
Baudissin 12	Brösa.............................14	Commerau
Bautzen 12	Brösang 29	bei Königswartha........9
Bederwitz......................21	Buchholz bei Bocka........7	Cortnitz 18
Belgern 18	Buchwalda......................15	Cosel im Gebirge.............21
Bellschwitz.....................21	Bürkau 8	Cossern 29
Belmsdorf 2	Burk 12	Crostau..........................22
Berge 21	Buscheritz......................8	Dahlowitz 16
Binnewitz 21	Buschermühle.................29	Dahren...........................8
Birkau 8	Callenberg 22	Daranitz 12
Birkenroda 29	Caminau	Demitz 30
Bischofswerda 2	bei Königswartha 10	Denkwitz 21
Bloaschütz.....................8	Caminau bei Radibor.......10	Diehmen 29
Blösa.............................12	Canitz Christina 19	Döberkütz.......................8

* not shown, belonged to the parish of Ponickau, AH Grossenhain

AMTSHAUPTMANNSCHAFT KAMENZ
LUTHERAN PARISHES

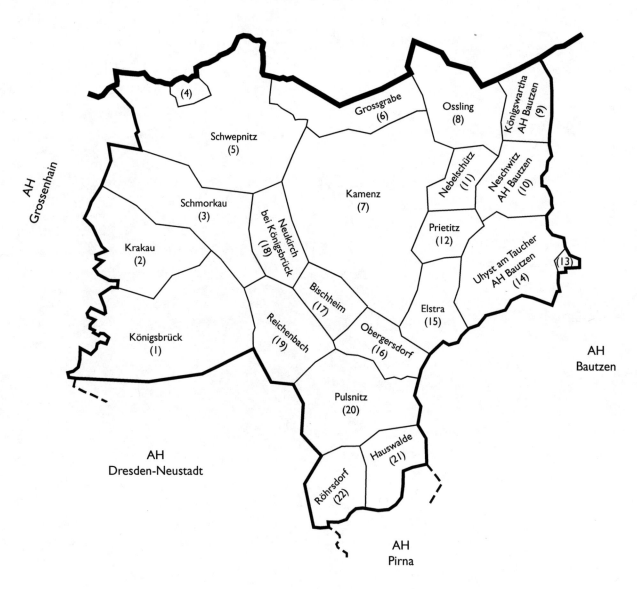

Province of Schlesien
Kingdom of Prussia

AH
Grossenhain

(4)

Schwepnitz
(5)

Grossgrabe
(6)

Ossling
(8)

Königswartha
AH Bautzen
(9)

Schmorkau
(3)

Neukirch
bei Königsbrück
(18)

Kamenz
(7)

Nebelschütz
(11)

Neschwitz
AH Bautzen
(10)

Krakau
(2)

Prietitz
(12)

Bischheim
(17)

Uhyst am Taucher
AH Bautzen
(14)

(13)

Königsbrück
(1)

Reichenbach
(19)

Obergersdorf
(16)

Elstra
(15)

AH
Bautzen

Pulsnitz
(20)

Hauswalde
(21)

AH
Dresden-Neustadt

Röhrsdorf
(22)

AH
Pirna

10 miles		20 miles	
10 km	20 km	30 km	

228

PARISH KEY

1. Königsbrück ....
2. Krakau ....
3. Schmorkau...................
4. Hermsdorf
   Province of Silesia
   Kingdom of Prussia .....
5. Schwepnitz ....
6. Grossgrabe.................
7. Kamenz.......................
8. Ossling........................
9. Königswartha
   AH Bautzen ....
10. Neschwitz
    AH Bautzen ....
11. Nebelschütz ....

12. Prietitz.......................
13. Göda
    AH Bautzen ....
14. Uhyst am Taucher
    AH Bautzen ....
15. Elstra.........................
16. Obergersdorf...............
17. Bischheim...................
18. Neukirch
    bei Königsbrück...........
19. Reichenbach ....
20. Pultznitz....................
21. Hauswalde ....
22. Röhrsdorf...................

TOWN KEY

Alte Ziegelscheune	10
Altenhain.......................	7
Auschkowitz...................	14
Berenbach	7
Bernbruch.....................	7
Biehla...........................	7
Bischheim.....................	17
Bocka...........................	14
Boderitz	15
Böhmisch......................	20
Böhmisch Bollung...........	20
Böhmische Folge.............	20
Bohra	2
Brauna	7
Brauschwitz...................	
Brautitz	
Bretnig	21
Bulleritz	7
Buschschenke	8
Camenz.........................	7
Cannewitz bei Marienstern...........	14
Caseritz	10
Cosel bei Königsbrück.....	5
Crostwitz......................	14

Cunnersdorf bei Kamenz..............	7
Cunnewitz bei Marienstern...........	9
Deutsch Baselitz.............	7
die Rothe Mühle	7
Döbra...........................	8
Dobrig	15
Dürrwicknitz	12
Elstra	15
Erlichtmühle bei Elstra.....	15
Forstmühle....................	6
Freihufe zu Neukirch	18
Friedersdorf	20
Gelenau........................	7
Glaubnitz	14
Glauschnitz....................	1
Gödlau	15
Göhlenau	7
Gottschdorf...................	18
Gränze	10
Grossgrabe....................	6
Grossröhrsdorf...............	22
Grossröhrsdorf bei Radeberg	

Grünberg	6
Grüngräbchen................	5
Hahnmühle	15
Haseldorf......................	
Hässlich	17
Hausdorf.......................	7
Hauswalde....................	21
Hennersdorf bei Kamenz................	7
Höckendorf	1
Höfgen..........................	
Höflein	14
Horka	10
Jauer............................	15
Jesau............................	7
Jiedlitz.........................	14
Kamenz	7
Kaschwitz	14
Kindisch	15
Kleinburkau...................	14
Kleinröhrsdorf	22
Kobschien.....................	
Koitsch.........................	18
Königsbrück...................	1
Kopschin.......................	

229

AMTSHAUPTMANNSCHAFT LÖBAU
LUTHERAN PARISHES

AH
Bautzen

Province of Schlesien
Kingdom of Prussia

(8)

Kotitz
(7)

(9)

Nostitz
(10)

Hochkirch
(6)

Kittlitz
(11)

(15)

Mittelsohland am Rotstein
(16)

Berzdorf auf dem Eigen
(19)

Cunewalde
(5)

Lawalde
(4)

Löbau
(12)

Bischdorf
(14)

Herwigsdorf
(13)

Kemnitz
(17)

(18)

Bernstadt auf dem Eigen
(20)

Obertaubenheim
(1)

(2)

(3)

Schönbach
(34)

Neusalza
(35)

(33)

Kottmarsdorf
(30)

(29)

Oberstrahwalde
(28)

Berthelsdorf
(23)

(22)

(21)

Spremberg
(36)

Ebersbach
(32)

(31)

Alteibau
(27)

Niederruppersdorf
(24)

Grosshennersdorf
(25)

Bohemia

Oberoderwitz
(26)

AH
Zittau

	10 miles		20 miles	
10 km		20 km	30 km	

PARISH KEY

TOWN KEY

233

AMTSHAUPTMANNSCHAFT ZITTAU
LUTHERAN PARISHES
After 1945 many of the cities on the eastern side of the district
came under Polish control.

Province of Schlesien
Kingdom of Prussia

AH
Löbau

Oberleuba
(14)

Nieda
(Silesia)
(15)

Grunau
(16)

Ostritz
(13)

Burkersdorf
(12)

Königshain
(17)

Mittelweigsdorf
(18)

Altgersdorf
(2)

Oberleutersdorf
(3)

(4)

Seifhennersdorf
(1)

(5)

Niederoderwitz
(7)

Oberseifersdorf
(9)

Hirschfelde
(11)

Wittgendorf
(10)

Türchau
(20)

Oberherwigsdorf
bei Zittau
(8)

Hainewalde
(6)

Reichenau
(19)

Grossschönau
(23)

(22)

Reibersdorf
(21)

Bohemia

Bertsdorf
(28)

(29)

Zittau
(25)

(24)

Jonsdorf
(27)

Lückendorf
(26)

Bohemia

10 miles		20 miles	
10 km	20 km	30 km	

PARISH KEY

TOWN KEY

238

Overview of districts, *Amtshauptmannschäfter*, in the
Kreishauptmannschaft Chemnitz
Kingdom of Saxony - Part II

KH
Leipzig
(Part I)

Duchy of
Saxe-Altenburg
(Thuringia)

AH
Flöha

AH
Freiberg

AH
Glauchau

AH
Chemnitz

AH
Stollberg

AH
Marienberg

KH
Zwickau
(Part I)

AH
Annaberg

Bohemia

AMTSHAUPTMANNSCHAFT ANNABERG
LUTHERAN PARISHES

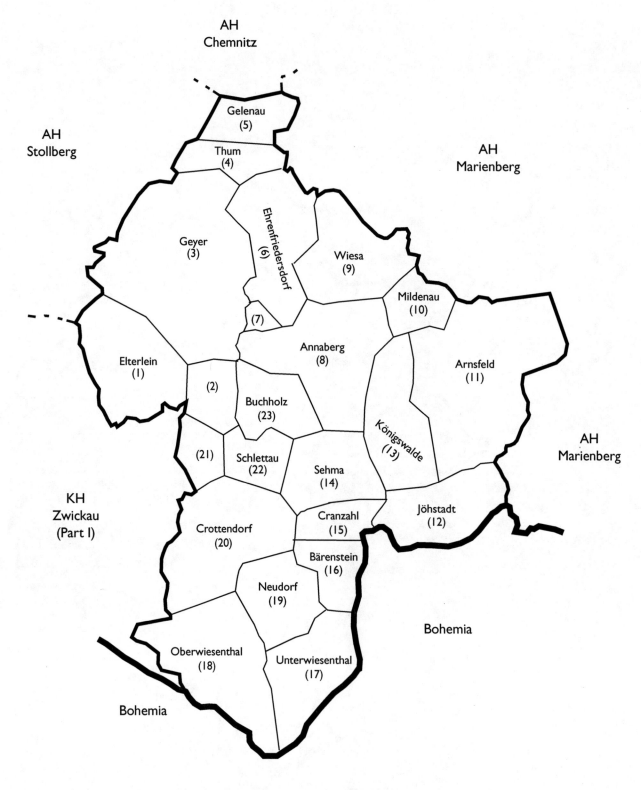

AH
Chemnitz

AH
Stollberg

AH
Marienberg

Gelenau
(5)

Thum
(4)

Geyer
(3)

Ehrenfriedersdorf
(6)

Wiesa
(9)

Mildenau
(10)

(7)

Annaberg
(8)

Arnsfeld
(11)

Elterlein
(1)

(2)

Buchholz
(23)

Königswalde
(13)

AH
Marienberg

(21)

Schlettau
(22)

Sehma
(14)

KH
Zwickau
(Part I)

Crottendorf
(20)

Cranzahl
(15)

Jöhstadt
(12)

Bärenstein
(16)

Neudorf
(19)

Bohemia

Oberwiesenthal
(18)

Unterwiesenthal
(17)

Bohemia

10 miles		20 miles	
10 km	20 km	30 km	

240

PARISH KEY

1.	Elterlein		13.	Königswalde ....
2.	Hermannsdorf 1271440		14.	Sehma 1271289
3.	Geyer		15.	Cranzahl.....................
4.	Thum..........................		16.	Bärenstein ....
5.	Gelenau......................		17.	Unterwiesenthal..........
6.	Ehrenfriedersdorf........		18.	Oberwiesenthal ....
7.	Tannenberg		19.	Neudorf......................
8.	Annaberg 73117		20.	Crottendorf ....
9.	Wiesa		21.	Scheibenberg ....
10.	Mildenau....................		22.	Schlettau ....
11.	Arnsfeld		23.	Buchholz....................
12.	Jöhstadt..................... 1271264			

TOWN KEY

Annaberg	8	Friedelmühle	11	Mildenau	10
Arnsfeld	11	Frohnau	8	Mittelschmiedeberg	11
Bärenlohe	17	Geiersberg	3	Naundorf	9
Bärenstein	16	Geiersdorf	8	Neudeck	8
Berggut	11	Gelenau	5	Neudorf	19
Berghäusel	12	Geyer	3	Neue Haus	17
Blumenhof	3	Grumbach	11	Neundorf	9
Bottendorfer Mühle	12	Grundmühle	16	Niederschlag	16
Brünnlastgüter	1	Hammermühle	7	Niederschmiedeberg	11
Buchholz	23	Hammerunterwiesenthal	17	Oberdorf	4
Buchwald	6	Hammer-		Oberndorf	4
Burgstädtel	1	Unterwiesenthal	17	Oberschaar	11
Buschmühle	5	Häuser am Kühberg	16	Oberscheibe	21
Cranzahl	15	Herrmannsdorf	2	Oberscheube	21
Crottendorf	20	Hohngut	11	Oberwiesenthal	18
Cunersdorf	14	Hünerkopf	8	Preishaus	17
Cunnersdorf	14	Jahnsbach	4	Raum	8
das Rothe Vorwerk	8	Jöhstadt	12	Raummühle	11
das Rothe Vorwerk	17	Kappelmühle	11	Reuterhaus	22
das Weise Vorwerk	17	Klappermühle	16	Rothenhammer	
das Weisse Gut	9	Kleinrückerswalde	8	bei Wiesenthal	17
der Raum	8	Königswalde	13	Sachsmüuhle	11
die Rothe Mühle	8	Kretzscham		Scheibe bei Frohnau	8
Dörfel	2	Rothensehma	19	Scheibenberg	21
Dorfmühle	11	Kretzschmar		Schlettau	22
Ehrenfriedersdorf	6	Rothensehma	19	Schlössel	12
Elterlein	1	Krottendorf	20	Schmalzgrube	11
Finsterau	10	Kühberg	16	Schönfeld	6
Förstel	1	Letzschmühle	7	Schützenhof	3
Forsthaus Kriegwald	15	Lotzschmühle	6	Sehma	14

AMTSHAUPTMANNSCHAFT CHEMNITZ
LUTHERAN PARISHES

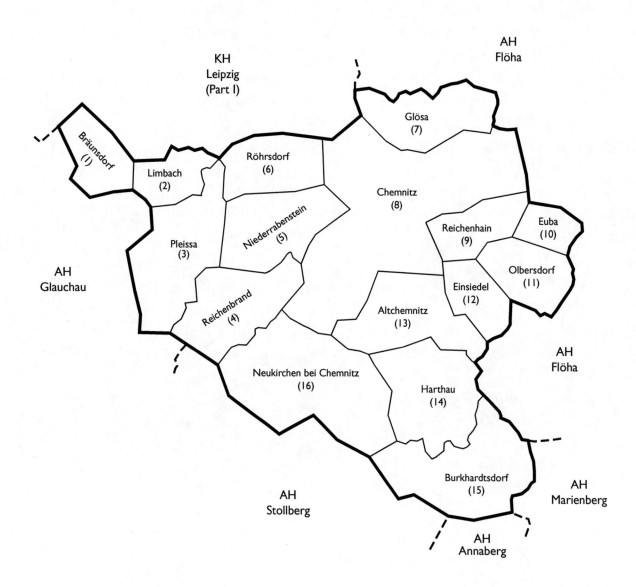

KH
Leipzig
(Part I)

AH
Flöha

Bräunsdorf
(1)

Limbach
(2)

Röhrsdorf
(6)

Glösa
(7)

Chemnitz
(8)

Reichenhain
(9)

Euba
(10)

Pleissa
(3)

Niederrabenstein
(5)

Olbersdorf
(11)

AH
Glauchau

Einsiedel
(12)

Reichenbrand
(4)

Altchemnitz
(13)

AH
Flöha

Neukirchen bei Chemnitz
(16)

Harthau
(14)

Burkhardtsdorf
(15)

AH
Marienberg

AH
Stollberg

AH
Annaberg

	10 miles		20 miles	
10 km		20 km	30 km	

244

PARISH KEY

TOWN KEY

AMTSHAUPTMANNSCHAFT FLÖHA
LUTHERAN PARISHES

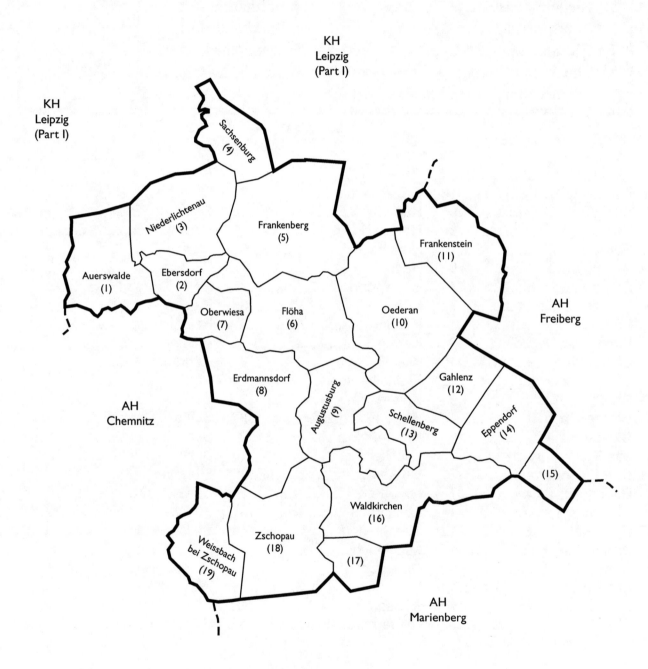

KH
Leipzig
(Part I)

KH
Leipzig
(Part I)

Sachsenburg
(4)

Niederlichtenau
(3)

Frankenberg
(5)

Frankenstein
(11)

AH
Freiberg

Auerswalde
(1)

Ebersdorf
(2)

Oberwiesa
(7)

Flöha
(6)

Oederan
(10)

Erdmannsdorf
(8)

Augustusburg
(9)

Gahlenz
(12)

Schellenberg
(13)

Eppendorf
(14)

AH
Chemnitz

(15)

Waldkirchen
(16)

Weissbach
bei Zschopau
(19)

Zschopau
(18)

(17)

AH
Marienberg

10 miles		20 miles	
10 km	20 km	30 km	

TOWN KEY

AMTSHAUPTMANNSCHAFT GLAUCHAU
LUTHERAN PARISHES

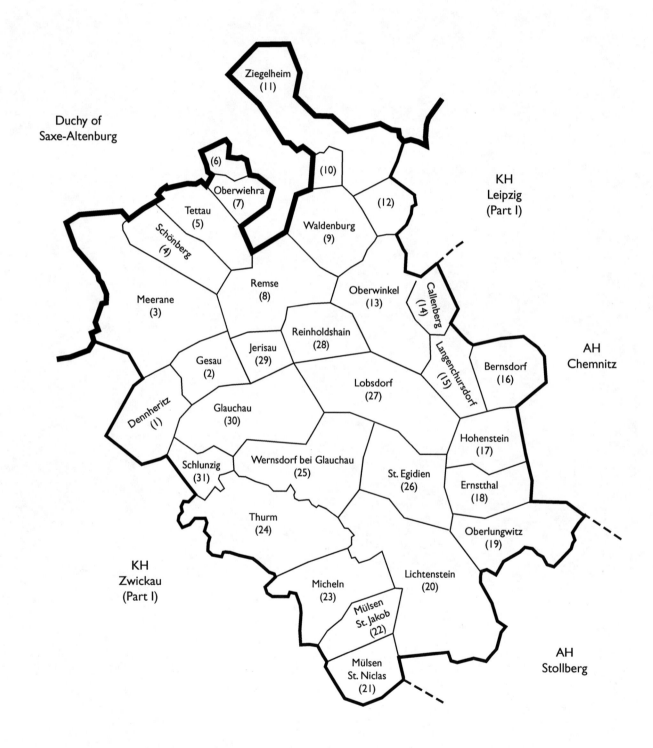

Ziegelheim
(11)

Duchy of
Saxe-Altenburg

KH
Leipzig
(Part I)

(6)

Oberwiehra
(7)

(10)

(12)

Tettau
(5)

Schönberg
(4)

Waldenburg
(9)

Meerane
(3)

Remse
(8)

Oberwinkel
(13)

Callenberg
(14)

AH
Chemnitz

Reinholdshain
(28)

Langenchursdorf
(15)

Jerisau
(29)

Gesau
(2)

Lobsdorf
(27)

Bernsdorf
(16)

Dennheritz
(1)

Glauchau
(30)

Hohenstein
(17)

Schlunzig
(31)

Wernsdorf bei Glauchau
(25)

St. Egidien
(26)

Ernstthal
(18)

Thurm
(24)

Oberlungwitz
(19)

KH
Zwickau
(Part I)

Micheln
(23)

Lichtenstein
(20)

Mülsen
St. Jakob
(22)

AH
Stollberg

Mülsen
St. Niclas
(21)

	5 miles		10 miles	
	5 km	10 km	15 km	

PARISH KEY

TOWN KEY

251

AMTSHAUPTMANNSCHAFT MARIENBERG
LUTHERAN PARISHES

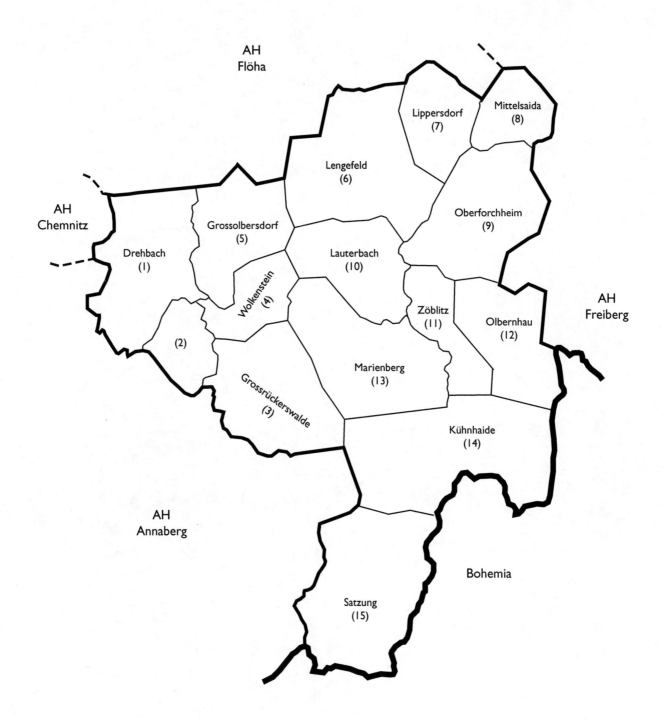

AH
Flöha

AH
Chemnitz

AH
Freiberg

AH
Annaberg

Lippersdorf
(7)

Mittelsaida
(8)

Lengefeld
(6)

Oberforchheim
(9)

Grossolbersdorf
(5)

Drehbach
(1)

Lauterbach
(10)

Wolkenstein
(4)

(2)

Zöblitz
(11)

Olbernhau
(12)

Marienberg
(13)

Grossrückerswalde
(3)

Kühnhaide
(14)

Bohemia

Satzung
(15)

	10 miles			20 miles	
10 km		20 km		30 km	

PARISH KEY

TOWN KEY

AMTSHAUPTMANNSCHAFT STOLLBERG
LUTHERAN PARISHES

AH
Glauchau

AH
Chemnitz

Ursprung
(4)

Erlbach
(3)

Lugau
(2)

Jahnsdorf
(6)

Oelsnitz
(1)

Stollberg
(5)

Thalheim
(7)

Hormersdorf
(8)

Dorfchemnitz
(9)

KH
Zwickau
(Part I)

Niederzwönitz
(10)

AH
Annaberg

Zwönitz
(11)

5 miles		10 miles	
5 km	10 km	15 km	

PARISH KEY

1. Oelsnitz......................		7. Thalheim....................	
2. Lugau...........................		8. Hormersdorf	
3. Erlbach.......................		9. Dorfchemnitz..............	
4. Ursprung....................		10. Niederzwönitz.............	
5. Stollberg		11. Zwönitz.....................	
6. Jahnsdorf...................			

TOWN KEY

Abtei-Oberlungwitz	4	Hormersdorf....................	8	Oberwürschnitz...............	5
Auerbach	8	Jahnsdorf......................	6	Oelsnitz........................	1
Brünlos	5	Kirchberg	3	Richtermühle	4
Dittersdorf...................	11	Kühnhaide	11	Schafflegen....................	1
Dorfchemnitz	9	Lugau...........................	2	Scherfmühle	5
Erlbach	3	Meinersdorf....................	6	Schlettheim...................	1
Gablenz	5	Mitteldorf.....................	5	Seifersdorf	4
Gornsdorf......................	7	Neusorge	1	Silbergrube	7
Gorusdorf......................	7	Neuwiese.......................	1	Stollberg	5
Günsdorf.......................	8	Niederdorf.....................	5	Tauschermühle	11
Haselbacher Mühle..........	11	Niederwürschnitz............	5	Thalheim.......................	7
Herrnmühle....................	11	Niederzwönitz.................	10	Ursprung.......................	4
Hirschgrundmühle	4	Oberdorf	5	Zwönitz	11
Hoheneck	5				

Overview of districts, *Amtshauptmannschäfter*, in the
Kreishauptmannschaft Dresden
Kingdom of Saxony - Part II

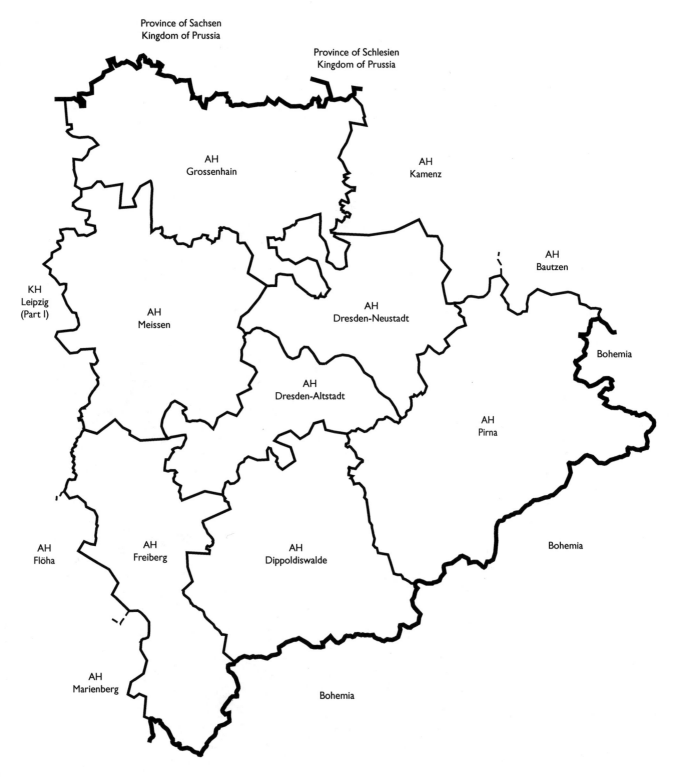

Province of Sachsen
Kingdom of Prussia

Province of Schlesien
Kingdom of Prussia

AH
Grossenhain

AH
Kamenz

AH
Bautzen

KH
Leipzig
(Part I)

AH
Meissen

AH
Dresden-Neustadt

Bohemia

AH
Dresden-Altstadt

AH
Pirna

AH
Flöha

AH
Freiberg

AH
Dippoldiswalde

Bohemia

AH
Marienberg

Bohemia

AMTSHAUPTMANNSCHAFT DIPPOLDISWALDE
LUTHERAN PARISHES

AH
Dresden-Altstadt

(9)

(8)

Possendorf
(10)

Kreischa
(11)

AH
Pirna

Höckendorf
(6)

Seifersdorf
bei Dippoldiswalde
(7)

Reinhardtsgrimma
(12)

Ruppendorf
(5)

Dippoldiswalde
(13)

Oberpretzschendorf
(3)

Reichstädt
(4)

Glashütte
(17)

(15)

Dittersdorf
(18)

Sadisdorf
(14)

Oberjohnsbach
(16)

Burkersdorf
(2)

(29)

Hennersdorf
(28)

Bärenstein
(24)

Liebenau
(19)

Frauenstein
(30)

Schönfeld
(27)

Schellerhau
(26)

Altenberg
(25)

Lauenstein
(23)

Dittersbach
(1)

AH
Freiberg

Nassau
(31)

Hermsdorf
(32)

Geising
(22)

Fürstenwalde
(20)

Fürstenau
(21)

Rechenberg
(33)

Bohemia

10 miles		20 miles	
10 km	20 km	30 km	

PARISH KEY

TOWN KEY

AMTSHAUPTMANNSCHAFT DRESDEN-ALTSTADT
LUTHERAN PARISHES

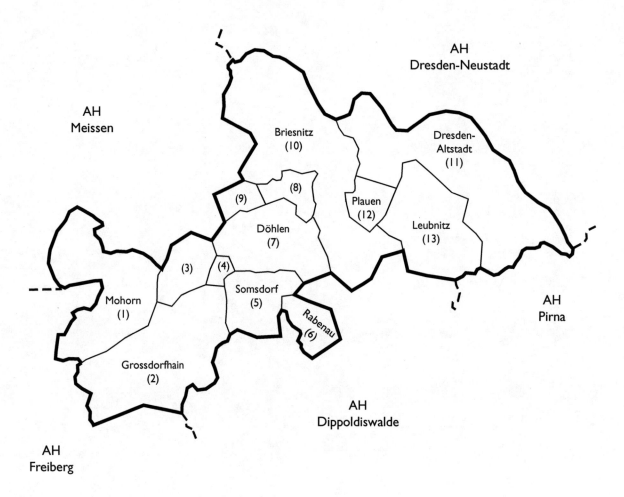

AH
Dresden-Neustadt

AH
Meissen

Briesnitz
(10)

Dresden-
Altstadt
(11)

(8)

(9)

Plauen
(12)

Döhlen
(7)

Leubnitz
(13)

(3)

(4)

Mohorn
(1)

Somsdorf
(5)

Rabenau
(6)

AH
Pirna

Grossdorfhain
(2)

AH
Dippoldiswalde

AH
Freiberg

	10 miles		20 miles	
10 km		20 km	30 km	

PARISH KEY

TOWN KEY

AMTSHAUPTMANNSCHAFT DRESDEN-NEUSTADT
LUTHERAN PARISHES

AH
Grossenhain

AH
Kamenz

AH
Meissen

Radeburg
(6)

(11)

Lomnitz
(10)

Ottendorf
(9)

Lichtenberg
(12)

Grünberg
(8)

Wachau
(13)

Kleinröhrsdorf
(15)

(5)

Lausa
(7)

Friedrichsthal
(14)

Reichenberg
(4)

Langebrück
(19)

Radeberg
(18)

Kötzschenbroda
(1)

Wallroda
(16)

Kaditz
(2)

Dresden-Neustadt
(3)

Kleinwolmsdorf
(17)

Weissig
bei Biehla
(21)

(20)

Loschwitz
(23)

Schönfeld
(22)

Hosterwitz
(24)

AH
Dresden-Altstadt

AH
Pirna

	10 miles			20 miles	
10 km		20 km		30 km	

PARISH KEY

TOWN KEY

271

AMTSHAUPTMANNSCHAFT FREIBERG
LUTHERAN PARISHES

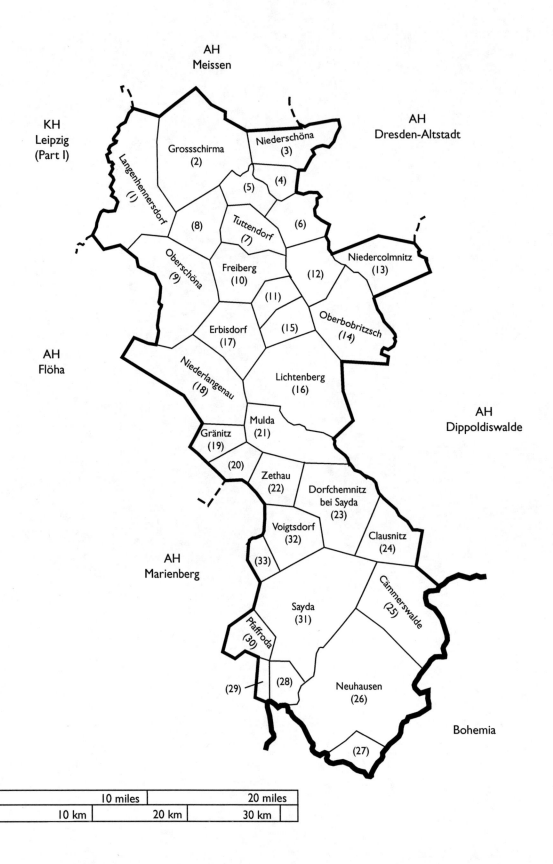

AH
Meissen

KH
Leipzig
(Part I)

AH
Dresden-Altstadt

Grossschirma
(2)

Niederschöna
(3)

Langenhennersdorf
(1)

(5)

(4)

(8)

Tuttendorf
(7)

(6)

Niedercolmnitz
(13)

Oberschöna
(9)

Freiberg
(10)

(12)

(11)

AH
Flöha

Erbisdorf
(17)

(15)

Oberbobritzsch
(14)

Niederlangenau
(18)

Lichtenberg
(16)

AH
Dippoldiswalde

Mulda
(21)

Gränitz
(19)

(20)

Zethau
(22)

Dorfchemnitz
bei Sayda
(23)

Voigtsdorf
(32)

Clausnitz
(24)

AH
Marienberg

(33)

Cämmerswalde
(25)

Sayda
(31)

Pfaffroda
(30)

(29)

(28)

Neuhausen
(26)

Bohemia

(27)

	10 miles		20 miles	
10 km	20 km		30 km	

PARISH KEY

1. Langenhennersdorf......		18. Niederlangenau............	
2. Grossschirma..............		19. Gränitz....................	
3. Niederschöna..............		20. Grosshartmannsdorf....	
4. Krummenhennersdorf..		21. Mulda....................	
5. Conradsdorf...............		22. Zethau....................	
6. Naundorf		23. Dorfchemnitz	
bei Tharandt...............		bei Sayda	
7. Tuttendorf..................		24. Clausnitz..................	
8. Kleinwaltersdorf..........		25. Cämmerswalde	
9. Oberschöna...............		26. Neuhausen	
10. Freiberg....................		27. Deutschneudorf...........	
11. Berthelsdorf...............		28. Oberneuschönberg.......	
12. Niederbobritzsch..........		29. Olbernhau	
13. Niedercolmnitz		AH Marienberg............	
14. Oberbobritzsch		30. Pfaffroda....................	
15. Weissenborn		31. Sayda	
16. Lichtenberg.................		32. Voigtsdorf	
17. Erbisdorf....................		33. Dörnthal....................	

TOWN KEY

Berthelsdorf...................11	Erlicht...........................3	Herrndorf 3	
Brand 17	Errlicht 3	Hetzdorf 3	
Bräunsdorf.....................1	Falkenberg.....................5	Hilbersdorf 5	
Brüderwiese..................26	Frauenbach 26	Hutha...........................30	
Cämmerswalde...............25	Fraunbach 26	Huthe............................3	
Catharinenberg...............27	Freiberg 10	Kleindittmannsdorf...........16	
Clausnitz........................24	Freibergsdorf 10	Kleinneuschönberg...........29	
Conradsdorf.....................5	Friedebach.....................31	Kleinschirma 9	
Crummenhennersdorf......4	Friedeburg 10	Kleinvoigtsberg 2	
das Rothe Vorwerk 10	Fürstenthal.....................10	Kleinwaltersdorf..............8	
der niedere Zug 10	Gränitz...........................19	Kohlung 2	
der obere Zug 10	Grosshartmannsdorf........20	Krummenhennersdorf......4	
Deutschcatharinenberg ...27	Grossschirma 2	Lampersdorf 14	
Deutscheinsiedel 26	Grossvoigtsberg 2	Langenhennersdorf 1	
Deutschgeorgenthal 25	Hallbach........................30	Langenrinne....................10	
Deutschneudorf 27	Hals 7	Lichtenberg.....................16	
Dittersbach 26	Halsbach........................5	Linda..............................9	
Dittmannsdorf bei Sayda .31	Halsbrücke......................7	Lossnitz 7	
Dorfchemnitz bei Sayda ..23	Hasenbrücke 25	Lössnitz 7	
Dörnthal........................33	Heidelbach......................26	Mönchenfrei 18	
Einsiedel 26	Heidelberg 26	Münchenfrei....................18	
Erbisdorf 17	Heidersdorf.....................31	Mulda............................21	

275

AMTSHAUPTMANNSCHAFT GROSSENHAIN
LUTHERAN PARISHES

Fichtenberg
Sachsen
(1)

(7)

(8)

Province of Sachsen
Kingdom of Prussia

Province of Schlesien
Kingdom of Prussia

(6)

Streumen
(5)

Frauenhain
(12)

Lorenzkirchen
(2)

(9)

Strauch
(15)

(17)

(19)

Linz
(20)

Ponickau
(22)

Gohlis
(3)

Peritz
(10)

Zabeltitz
(11)

Skässchen
(14)

Oelsnitz
(16)

KH
Leipzig
(Part I)

Zeithain
(4)

Walda
(13)

Bauda
(41)

Schönfeld
(21)

Lampertswalde
(18)

Glaubitz
(42)

Sacka
(23)

AH
Kamenz

Riesa
(44)

(40)

Hain
(37)

Heyda
(43)

(39)

Skassa
(38)

Reinersdorf
(32)

Dobra
(24)

Striesen
(36)

Lenz
(33)

Niederebersbach
(30)

Rödern
(28)

(25)

Seusslitz
(35)

(31)

Medingen
(26)

Wantewitz
(34)

AH
Meissen

Naunhof
(29)

Bärnsdorf
(27)

AH
Dresden-Neustadt

	10 miles		20 miles	
10 km		20 km		30 km

PARISH KEY

1. Fichtenberg
   Province of Sachsen
   Kingdom of Prussia.....
2. Lorenzkirchen...............
3. Gohlis ....
4. Zeithain...................
5. Streumen..................
6. Spansberg ....
7. Kröbeln
   Province of Sachsen
   Kingdom of Prussia.....
8. Stolzenhain
   Province of Sachsen
   Kingdom of Prussia.....
9. Koselitz.....................
10. Peritz.......................
11. Zabeltitz...................
12. Frauenhain.................
13. Walda.......................
14. Skässchen ....
15. Strauch.....................
16. Oelsnitz....................
17. Grossthiemig
    Province of Sachsen
    Kingdom of Prussia.....
18. Lampertswalde ....
19. Grosskmehlen
    Province of Sachsen
    Kingdom of Prussia.....
20. Linz..........................
21. Schönfeld...................
22. Ponickau ....
23. Sacka........................
24. Dobra ....
25. Würschnitz.................
26. Medingen...................
27. Bärnsdorf...................
28. Rödern ....
29. Naunhof....................
30. Niederebersbach ....
31. Grossdobritz
    AH Meissen...............
32. Reinersdorf.................
33. Lenz ....
34. Wantewitz ....
35. Seusslitz....................
36. Striesen ....
37. Hain ....
38. Skassa 1190917
39. Merschwitz ....
40. Wildenhain..................
41. Bauda.........................
42. Glaubitz ....
43. Heyda bei Riesa........... 73120
    1273369
44. Riesa ....

TOWN KEY

AMTSHAUPTMANNSCHAFT MEISSEN
LUTHERAN PARISHES

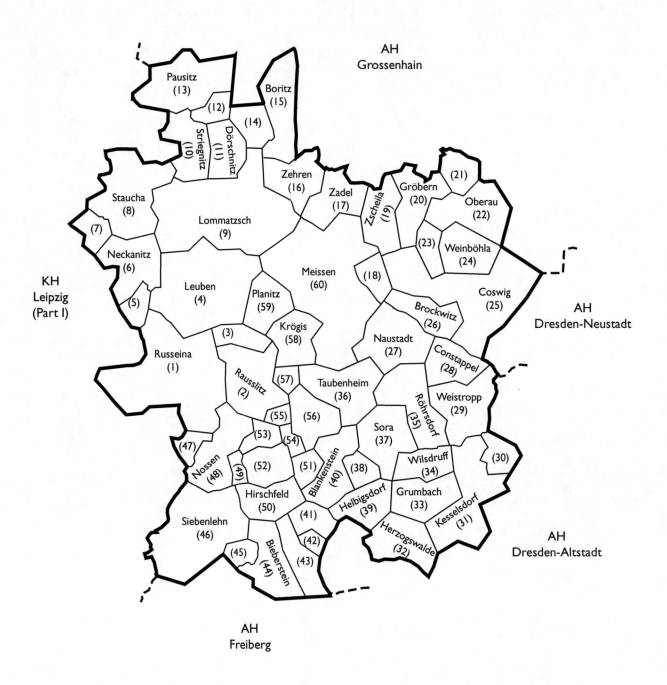

AH
Grossenhain

Pausitz
(13)

(12)

Boritz
(15)

(14)

Striegnitz
(10)

Dörschnitz
(11)

Zehren
(16)

Zadel
(17)

Zscheila
(19)

Gröbern
(20)

(21)

Oberau
(22)

Staucha
(8)

(7)

Lommatzsch
(9)

(23)

Weinböhla
(24)

Neckanitz
(6)

Meissen
(60)

(18)

Coswig
(25)

KH
Leipzig
(Part I)

(5)

Leuben
(4)

Planitz
(59)

Brockwitz
(26)

AH
Dresden-Neustadt

(3)

Krögis
(58)

Naustadt
(27)

Constappel
(28)

Russeina
(1)

Rausslitz
(2)

(57)

Taubenheim
(36)

Röhrsdorf
(35)

Weistropp
(29)

(55)

(56)

Sora
(37)

(30)

(47)

(53)

(54)

(51)

Blankenstein
(40)

(38)

Wilsdruff
(34)

Nossen
(48)

(49)

(52)

Hirschfeld
(50)

Helbigsdorf
(39)

Grumbach
(33)

Kesselsdorf
(31)

Siebenlehn
(46)

(45)

Bieberstein
(44)

(41)

(42)

(43)

Herzogswalde
(32)

AH
Dresden-Altstadt

AH
Freiberg

10 miles		20 miles	
10 km	20 km	30 km	

PARISH KEY

1. Rüsseina.....................
2. Rausslitz ....
3. Ziegenhain ....
4. Leuben ....
5. Beicha ....
6. Neckanitz ....
7. Zschochau...................
8. Staucha ....
9. Lommatzsch ....
10. Striegnitz.....................
11. Dörschnitz...................
12. Prausitz ....
13. Pausitz ....
14. Heyda bei Reisa
    AH Grossenhain 73120
    1273369
15. Boritz ....
16. Zehren.....................
17. Zadel.....................
18. Cölln an der Elbe ....
19. Zscheila.....................
20. Gröbern.....................
21. Grossdobritz ....
22. Oberau ....
23. Niederau ....
24. Weinböhla...................
25. Coswig.....................
26. Brockwitz ....
27. Naustadt...................
28. Constappel ....
29. Weisstropp ....
30. Unckersdorf.................

31. Kesselsdorf ....
32. Herzogswalde ....
33. Grumbach ....
34. Wilsdruff...................
35. Röhrsdorf...................
36. Taubenheim ....
37. Sora.....................
38. Limbach...................
39. Helbigsdorf.................
40. Blankenstein ....
41. Neukirchen
    bei Meissen...............
42. Dittmannsdorf.............
43. Oberreinsberg ....
44. Bieberstein...................
45. Obergruna.................
46. Siebenlehn ....
47. Gleisberg
    AH Döbeln.................
48. Nossen ....
49. Niedereula.................
50. Hirschfeld ....
51. Alttanneberg ....
52. Deutschenbora.............
53. Wendischbora ....
54. Rothschönberg............
55. Heinitz ....
56. Burkhardtswalde.........
57. Miltitz ....
58. Krögis ....
59. Planitz.....................
60. Meissen...................

TOWN KEY

Abend 1	Alt Zaschendorf 18	Alttanneberg 51
Albertitz.................... 6	Althöfchen.................... 1	Arntitz 8
Alt Choren.................... 1	Althöffchen.................... 1	Augustusberg 48
Alt Hirschstein.................... 15	Altrobschütz.................... 60	Badersen 4
Alt Lommatzsch 9	Altsattel.................... 8	Bahra.................... 15

283

AMTSHAUPTMANNSCHAFT PIRNA
LUTHERAN PARISHES

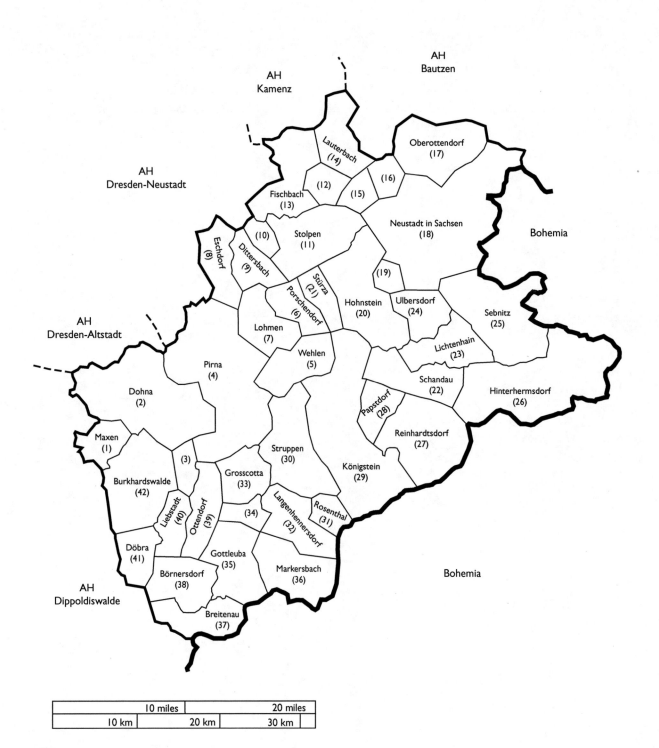

AH
Kamenz

AH
Bautzen

AH
Dresden-Neustadt

Lauterbach
(14)

Oberottendorf
(17)

(12)

(16)

Fischbach
(13)

(15)

Bohemia

Eschdorf
(8)

(10)

Stolpen
(11)

Neustadt in Sachsen
(18)

Dittersbach
(9)

Stürza
(21)

(19)

AH
Dresden-Altstadt

Porschendorf
(6)

Hohnstein
(20)

Ulbersdorf
(24)

Sebnitz
(25)

Lohmen
(7)

Lichtenhain
(23)

Pirna
(4)

Wehlen
(5)

Schandau
(22)

Hinterhermsdorf
(26)

Dohna
(2)

Papstdorf
(28)

Reinhardtsdorf
(27)

Maxen
(1)

Struppen
(30)

Königstein
(29)

(3)

Burkhardswalde
(42)

Grosscotta
(33)

Langenhennersdorf
(32)

Rosenthal
(31)

Liebstadt
(40)

Ottendorf
(39)

(34)

Döbra
(41)

Gottleuba
(35)

Börnersdorf
(38)

Markersbach
(36)

Bohemia

AH
Dippoldiswalde

Breitenau
(37)

10 miles		20 miles	
10 km	20 km	30 km	

PARISH KEY

TOWN KEY

CATHOLIC
PARISHES

Overview of districts, *Amtshauptmannschäfter*, in the
Kreishauptmannschaft Bautzen
Kingdom of Saxony - Part II

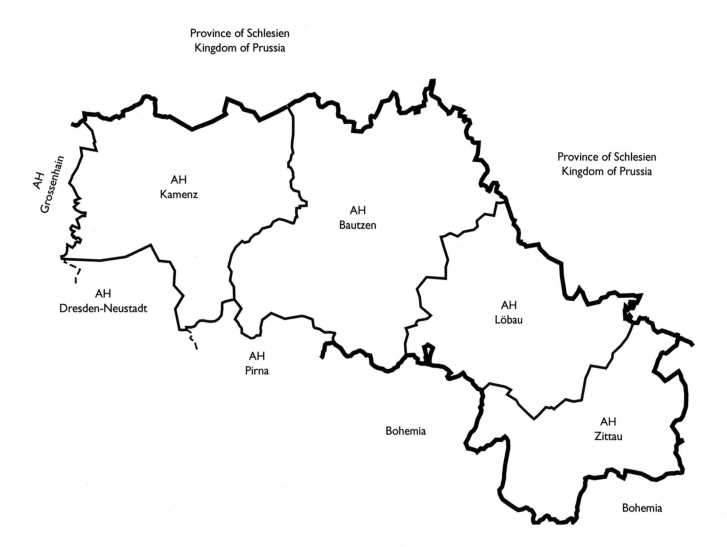

Province of Schlesien
Kingdom of Prussia

Province of Schlesien
Kingdom of Prussia

AH
Grossenhain

AH
Kamenz

AH
Bautzen

AH
Löbau

AH
Dresden-Neustadt

AH
Pirna

Bohemia

AH
Zittau

Bohemia

AMTSHAUPTMANNSCHAFT BAUTZEN
CATHOLIC PARISHES

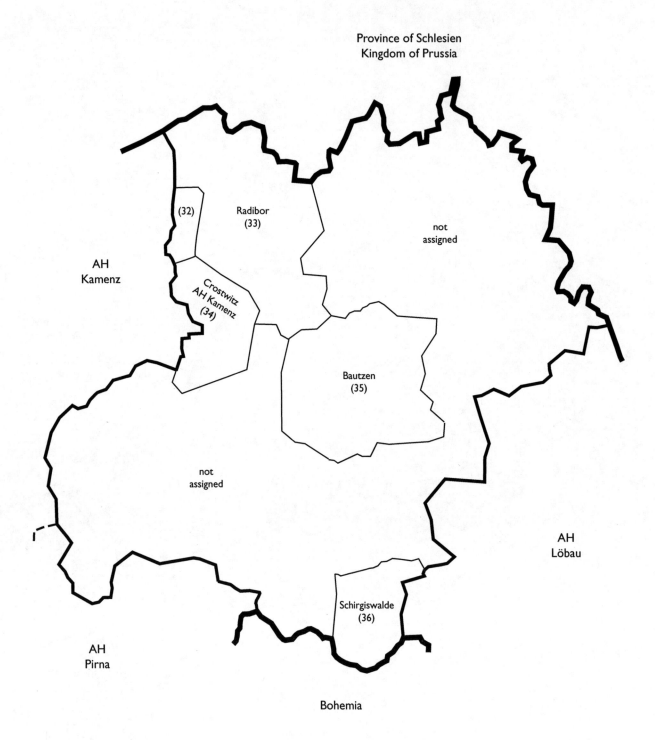

Province of Schlesien
Kingdom of Prussia

(32)

Radibor
(33)

not
assigned

AH
Kamenz

Crostwitz
AH Kamenz
(34)

Bautzen
(35)

not
assigned

AH
Löbau

Schirgiswalde
(36)

AH
Pirna

Bohemia

10 miles | 20 miles
10 km | 20 km | 30 km

TOWN KEY

* not shown - belonged to the parish of Ostro, AH Kamenz FHL film #1812917.

AMTSHAUPTMANNSCHAFT KAMENZ
CATHOLIC PARISHES

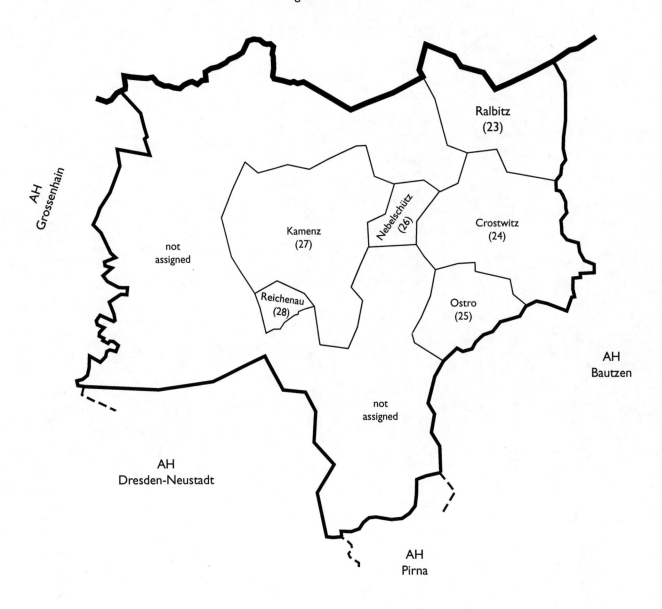

Province of Schlesien
Kingdom of Prussia

Ralbitz
(23)

AH
Grossenhain

Kamenz
(27)

not
assigned

Nebelschütz
(26)

Crostwitz
(24)

Reichenau
(28)

Ostro
(25)

not
assigned

AH
Bautzen

AH
Dresden-Neustadt

AH
Pirna

10 miles		20 miles	
10 km	20 km	30 km	

AMTSHAUPTMANNSCHAFT LÖBAU
CATHOLIC PARISHES

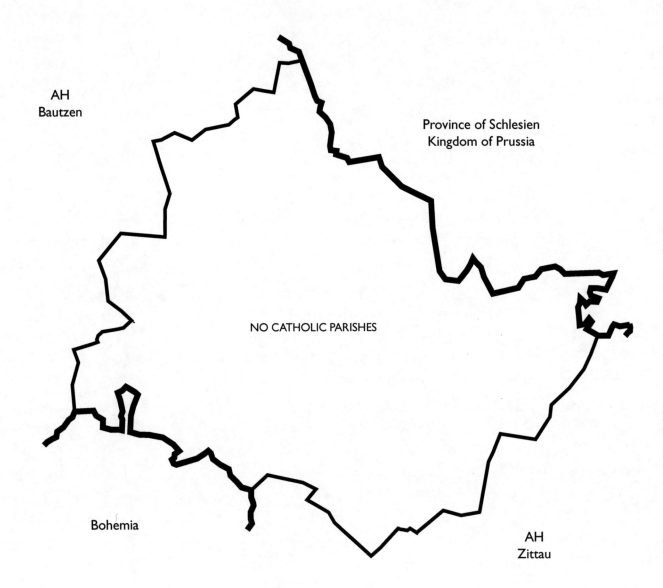

AH
Bautzen

Province of Schlesien
Kingdom of Prussia

NO CATHOLIC PARISHES

Bohemia

AH
Zittau

	10 miles		20 miles	
10 km		20 km	30 km	

TOWN KEY

Alt Bernsdorf....................

Altcunnewitz ....

Alteibau...........................

Beiersdorf bei Neusalza ..

Belbitz............................

Bellwitz ....

Bernstadt
    auf dem Eigen ....

Berthelsdorf ....

Berzdorf...........................

Berzdorf auf dem Eigen...

Bischdorf.........................

Blauer Stern.....................

Breitendorf ....

Buda ....

Carlsbrunn ....

Cränzmühle ....

Cunewald..........................

Cunnersdorf
    auf dem Eigen ....

Cunnewitz
    bei Marienstern..........

der blaue Stern ....

Dittersbach
    auf dem Eigen ....

Doigowitz.........................

Drauschwitz.....................

Dürrhennersdorf ....

Ebersbach ....

Ebersdorf.........................

Eiserode auf dem Eigen ..

Euldorf ....

Feldhäuser.......................

Feldschönau....................

Fichtelschenke................

Friedensthal.....................

Fritzkau...........................

Georgewitz ....

Glossen ....

Gosswitz..........................

Grossdehsa ....

Grosshennersdorf............

Grossschweidnitz ....

Grosstrebnitz ....

Grube...............................

Haine ....

Halbau ....

Halbe ....

Hempel ....

Henschenne ....

Herrnhut...........................

Herwigsdorf bei Löbau.....

Hochkirch.........................

Hohkirch ....

Jauernick ....

Joachimstein....................

Kalkreuth ....

Kemnitz............................

Kerbisdorf ....

Kiebnitz............................

Kiesdorf auf dem Eigen ...

Kittlitz...............................

Kleindehsa.......................

Kleinradmeritz..................

Kleinschweidnitz..............

Kleintetta.........................

Klipphausen.....................

Klipphäuser......................

Köblitz.............................

Kohlwesa ....

Körbigsdorf ....

Kotitz................................

Kottmarhäuser ....

Kottmarsdorf....................

Kötzschau ....

Kötzsche ....

Krappe ....

Kuppritz ....

Langhennersdorf ....

Lauba...............................

Laucha ....

Lauske bei Hochkirch ......

Lautitz..............................

Lawalde ....

Lehn bei Hochkirch..........

Liebesdörfel.....................

Lindenberg.......................

Löbau...............................

Maltitz..............................

Mauschwitz......................

Mengelsdorfer Mühle.......

Mittelcunewalde...............

Mittelfreidersdorf.............

Mittelherwigsdorf ....

Mittelrosenhain ....

Mittelsohland
    am Rotstein ....

Necheu ....

Neuberthelsdorf..............

Neucunnersdorf..............

Neucunnewitz ....

Neudorf............................

Neudorf bei Lauba ....

Neudorf bei Schönbach...

Neudörfel
    bei Cunewalde............

Neue Häuser ....

Neue Schenke.................

Neueibau ....

Neufriedersdorf...............

Neuhof.............................

Neukotitz..........................

Neulauba ....

Neulindenberg ....

Neundorf..........................

Neuoppach ....

Neusalza...........................

Neuschönberg ....

Neuspreedorf...................

Neuspremberg..................

Neutaubenheim ....

Nieder Herwigsdorf..........

Niederbeiersdorf..............

Niederbelbitz....................

Niederberthelsdorf..........

Niederbischdorf ....

AMTSHAUPTMANNSCHAFT ZITTAU
CATHOLIC PARISHES
After 1945 some of the cities on the eastern side of the district came under Polish control.

Province of Schlesien
Kingdom of Prussia

AH
Löbau

Grunau
(35)

Ostritz
(34)

Königshain
(33)

Neuleutersdorf
(30)

not
assigned

Seitendorf
(32)

not
assigned

Zittau
(31)

Bohemia

Bohemia

10 miles		20 miles	
10 km	20 km	30 km	

Overview of districts, *Amtshauptmannschäfter*, in the
Kreishauptmannschaft Chemnitz
Kingdom of Saxony - Part II

KH
Leipzig
(Part I)

Duchy of
Saxe-Altenburg
(Thuringia)

AH
Flöha

AH
Freiberg

AH
Glauchau

AH
Chemnitz

AH
Stollberg

AH
Marienberg

KH
Zwickau
(Part I)

AH
Annaberg

Bohemia

AMTSHAUPTMANNSCHAFT ANNABERG
CATHOLIC PARISHES

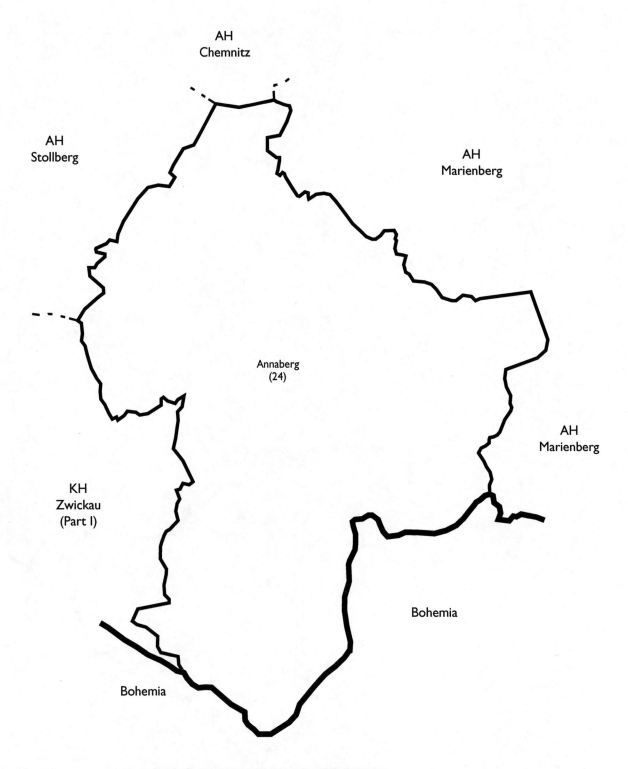

AH
Chemnitz

AH
Stollberg

AH
Marienberg

Annaberg
(24)

AH
Marienberg

KH
Zwickau
(Part I)

Bohemia

Bohemia

	10 miles		20 miles	
10 km		20 km	30 km	

PARISH KEY

TOWN KEY

AMTSHAUPTMANNSCHAFT CHEMNITZ
CATHOLIC PARISHES

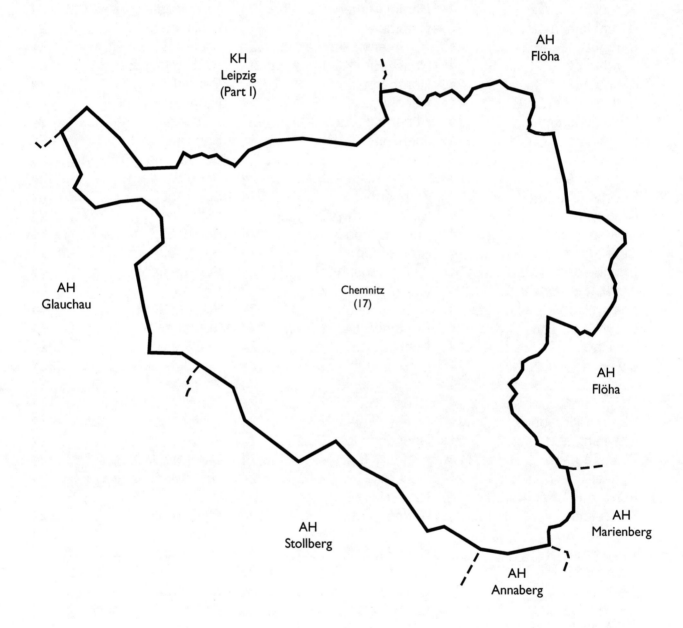

KH
Leipzig
(Part I)

AH
Flöha

AH
Glauchau

Chemnitz
(17)

AH
Flöha

AH
Marienberg

AH
Stollberg

AH
Annaberg

	10 miles		20 miles	
	10 km	20 km	30 km	

PARISH KEY

17. Chemnitz...................... 1812921

TOWN KEY

AMTSHAUPTMANNSCHAFT FLÖHA
CATHOLIC PARISHES

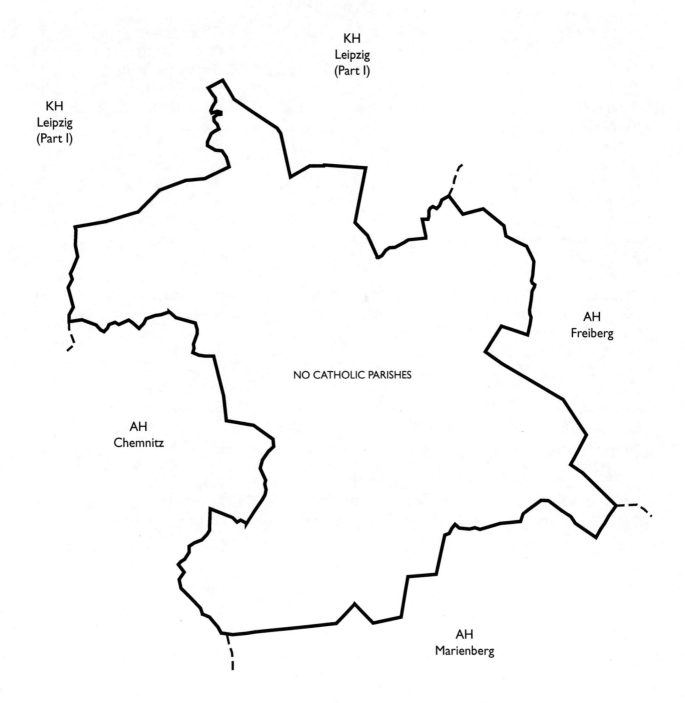

KH
Leipzig
(Part I)

KH
Leipzig
(Part I)

AH
Freiberg

NO CATHOLIC PARISHES

AH
Chemnitz

AH
Marienberg

	10 miles		20 miles	
10 km		20 km	30 km	

NO CATHOLIC PARISHES

TOWN KEY

Altenhain......................	Grünberg	Niederlichtenau...............
Auerswalde...................	Grünhainichen	Niedermühlbach ....
Augustusburg	Gückelsberg	Niederwiesa...................
Beisorge	Gunnersdorf...................	Oberauerswalde ....
Bernsdorf.....................	Hammermühle................	Obergarnsdorf ....
Biensdorf	Hartha..........................	Oberlichtenau ....
Börnchen	Hausdorf.......................	Obermühlbach ....
Börnichen bei Oederan....	Hausdorf.......................	Oberwiesa ....
Börnichen bei Zschorau...	Heiersdorf.....................	Oederan........................
Borstendorf...................	Hennersdorf	Oertelsdorf....................
Braunsdorf....................	Hessdorf	Ortelsdorf.....................
Bräunsdorf....................	Hintermühle	Plaue ....
Breitenau	Hohe Fichte	Porschendorf ....
Brückengut	Hohe Linde	Richtermühle ....
Cunnersdorf...................	Hohenfichte	Sachsenburg ....
Dammmühle	Hohenlinde	Schellenberg..................
Dittersbach	Höllenmühle...................	Schlösschen ....
Dittersdorf....................	Irbersdorf	Schlösselmühle ....
Dittmannsdorf	Jägerhof........................	Schönborn ....
Dorfschellenberg	Kirchbach......................	Schönerstadt ....
Dreiwerden	Kleinhartmannsdorf	Schwarzmühle ....
Ebersbach	Krumhermersdorf............	Schwedei......................
Ebersdorf.....................	Kunnersdorf...................	Schwettei......................
Eppendorf.....................	Leubsdorf......................	Stegvorwerk...................
Erdmannsdorf................	Lichtenwalde..................	Tannenmühle ....
Falkenau......................	Lichtewalde...................	Thiemendorf ....
Finkenburg....................	Marbach........................	Waldkirchen...................
Fischhaus	Memmendorf	Weissbach
Flöha...........................	Merzdorf	bei Zschopau ....
Flossmühle	Metzdorf........................	Wilischthal ....
Frankenberg	Mühlbach.......................	Wingendorf ....
Frankenstein..................	Neubau.........................	Witzschdorf....................
Gahlenz	Neudörfchen	Witzschendorf.................
Garnsdorf.....................	bei Sachsenburg.........	Wolfsberg bei Neusorge ..
Görbersdorf	Neunzehnhain	Zschopau......................
Gornau........................	Nieder Auerswalde	Zschopenthal ....
Grosswaltersdorf	Niedergarnsdorf.............	

AMTSHAUPTMANNSCHAFT GLAUCHAU
CATHOLIC PARISHES

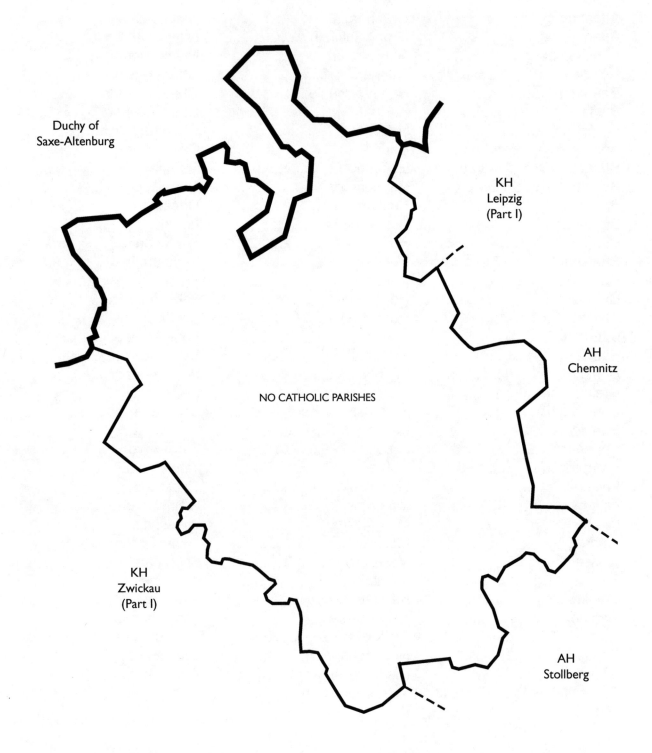

Duchy of
Saxe-Altenburg

KH
Leipzig
(Part I)

AH
Chemnitz

NO CATHOLIC PARISHES

KH
Zwickau
(Part I)

AH
Stollberg

	5 miles		10 miles	
	5 km	10 km	15 km	

TOWN KEY

Albertsthal......................	Hohenstein	Rectormühle ....
Altstadt-Waldenburg	Hohndorf.........................	Reichbach........................
Alt-Waldenburg	Holzhäuser	Reichenbach
au dem Wehricht	Hüttenmühle	bei Hohenstein...........
Bernsdorf	Jähsnitz	Reinholdshain.................
Bernstein	Jerisau	Remissen........................
Berthelsdorf	Jüdenhain	Remse ....
Breitenbach	Kertzsch..........................	Rödlitz.............................
Calinberg	Kleinbernsdorf	Rothenbach ....
Callenberg	Kleinchursdorf.................	Rudolphsmühle...............
Cauritz...........................	Kleinrümpf	Rümpf.............................
Crotenlaide	Köthel	Rüsdorf............................
Dennheritz	Kuhschnappel..................	Rüssdorf ....
Dietrich	Langenberg	Sankt Egidien ....
Dittrich	Langenchursdorf.............	Schäller...........................
Dürrenuhlsdorf.................	Lichtenstein	Schiefermühle.................
Ebersbach	Lipprandis	Schlunzig ....
Eichlaide........................	Lobsdorf..........................	Schönberg ....
Elzenberg	Ludwigsdorf	Schönbörnchen ....
Engelmühle......................	Meerana	Schönbörngen ....
Ernstthal	Meinsdorf	Schwaben........................
Falken............................	Micheln	Seiferitz...........................
Franken	Mülsen St. Jacob	Stangendorf.....................
Frankenhof	Mülsen St. Michaelis.......	Tempel............................
Gässnitz..........................	Mülsen St. Niclas............	Tettau..............................
Gesau............................	Niederarnsdorf................	Thiergarten ....
Glauchau	Niederlungwitz	Thurm..............................
Gränzmühle......................	Niedermülsen	Tirschheim ....
Greenfield.......................	Niederwinkel	Trützschler ....
Grossrümpf......................	Nutzung	Uhlmannsdorf ....
Grünfeld..........................	Oberdorf	Voigtlaide.........................
Grumbach........................	Oberlungwitz....................	Waldenburg ....
Harthau..........................	Oberndorf	Weidensdorf ....
Haublermühle	Oberschindmaas	Weinwiese ....
Häuslermühle	Oberwiehra	Wernsdorf bei Glauchau..
Heickendorf	Oberwiera	Wickersdorf
Heiersdorf	Oberwinkel.......................	(Sachsen section).......
(Saxony section)........	Oberwyhra	Wünschendorf ....
Hermsdorf........................	Oertelshain	Ziegelheim ....
Höckendorf	Pfaffroda	Ziegeluhlsdorf.................

321

AMTSHAUPTMANNSCHAFT MARIENBERG
CATHOLIC PARISHES

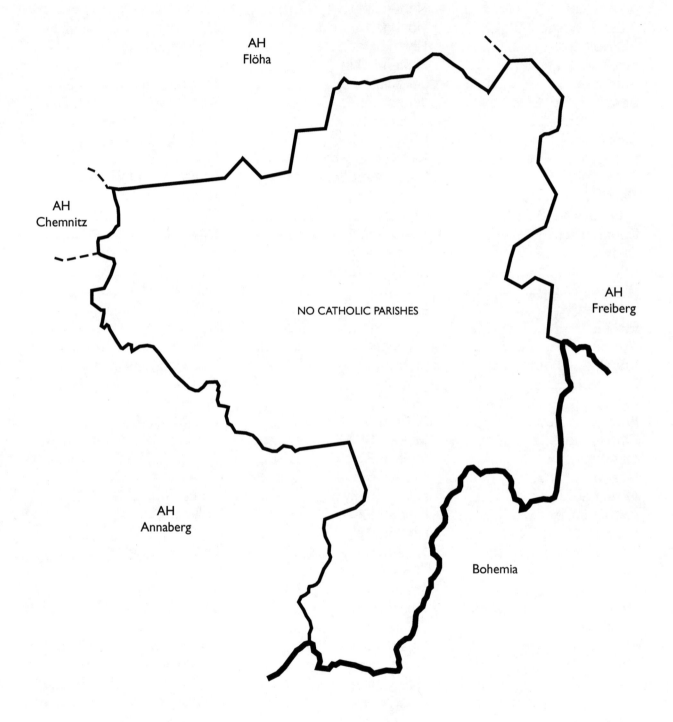

AH
Flöha

AH
Chemnitz

NO CATHOLIC PARISHES

AH
Freiberg

AH
Annaberg

Bohemia

10 miles | 20 miles
10 km | 20 km | 30 km

TOWN KEY

Ansprung ....
Baademühle ....
Blumenau ....
Bobershau ....
Bockau..........................
Boden mit Schindelbach..
Bodenmühle ....
Brechhaus ....
Dammmühle ....
das Rothe Haus..............
der Rothe Pfütze.....
der Weisse Hirsch ....
Dörfel..............................
Drachenwald...................
Drebach ....
Drehbach.......................
Einsiedel-
    Senfenhammer ....
Eschenbach
    bei Wolkenstein ....
Falkenbach ....
Fernrückerswalde............
Fischhaus ....
Flosslohnhaus
    bei Görsdorf...............
Forsthaus Grünthal..........
Forsthaus Heidelbach......
Gebirge............................
Gelobtes Land ....
Gerinswalde....................
Gersdorf..........................
Görsdorf..........................
Griesbach ....
Griesbachmühle ....
Griessbach ....
Grossolbersdorf..............
Grossrückerswalde..........
Grünau............................
Grünthal..........................
Grundau..........................
Hahngut..........................
Haingut............................

Hainzbauk......................
Haubolds Pulvermühle
    bei Olbernhau ....
Heinzebank......................
Heinzwaldmühle ....
Herold..............................
Hilmersdorf ....
Himmelmühle...................
Hirschberg ....
Hirschleitmühle ....
Hirschstein......................
Hohndorf..........................
Hölzelmühle.....................
Hopfgarten.......................
Hüttengrund.....................
Hüttengrundmühle ....
Huth..................................
Jädenhain ....
Jüdenhain........................
Karnmühle ....
Karrenmühle
    bei Rittersberg ....
Klatzschmühle ....
Kleinemühle.....................
Kohlau ....
Kohlmühle........................
Kühnhaide ....
Kupferhammer
    in Hüttengrunde ....
Laute................................
Lauterbach.......................
Leibnitzdörschen ....
Leibnitzdörschen Mühle...
Lengefeld.........................
Lippersdorf......................
Marienberg ....
Marterbüschel..................
Mittelsaida ....
Nennigmühle ....
Neudeck ....
Neuhaselbach..................
Neuhausmühle ....

Neumühle ....
Neusorge.........................
Niederdrehbach..............
Niederforchheim ....
Niederhaselbach..............
Niederlauterstein ....
Niedernatzschkau............
Niedernatzschung............
Niedersaida ....
Niederschindelbach ....
Niederseida ....
Oberdrehbach..................
Oberforchheim.................
Oberhaselbach ....
Obernatzschkau ....
Obernatzschung ....
Obersaida ....
Oberschindelbach............
Oberschmiedeberg..........
Oberseida ....
Olbernhau........................
Pobershau ....
Pockau.............................
Rauenstein ....
Reifland ....
Reissigmühle ....
Reitzenhain......................
Rittersberg ....
Rothenthal ....
Rübenau ....
Rückerswalde..................
Saigerhütte Grünthal ....
Satzung ....
Scharfenstein...................
Scheibe
    bei Schönbrunn ....
Scheibenmühle................
Scheidebach ....
Schickenmühle ....
Schindelbach ....
Schlettemühle ....
Schlossmühle ....

AMTSHAUPTMANNSCHAFT STOLLBERG
CATHOLIC PARISHES

AH
Glauchau

AH
Chemnitz

NO CATHOLIC PARISHES

KH
Zwickau
(Part I)

AH
Annaberg

	5 miles		10 miles	
5 km		10 km	15 km	

TOWN KEY

Overview of districts, *Amtshauptmannschäfter*, in the
Kreishauptmannschaft Dresden
Kingdom of Saxony - Part II

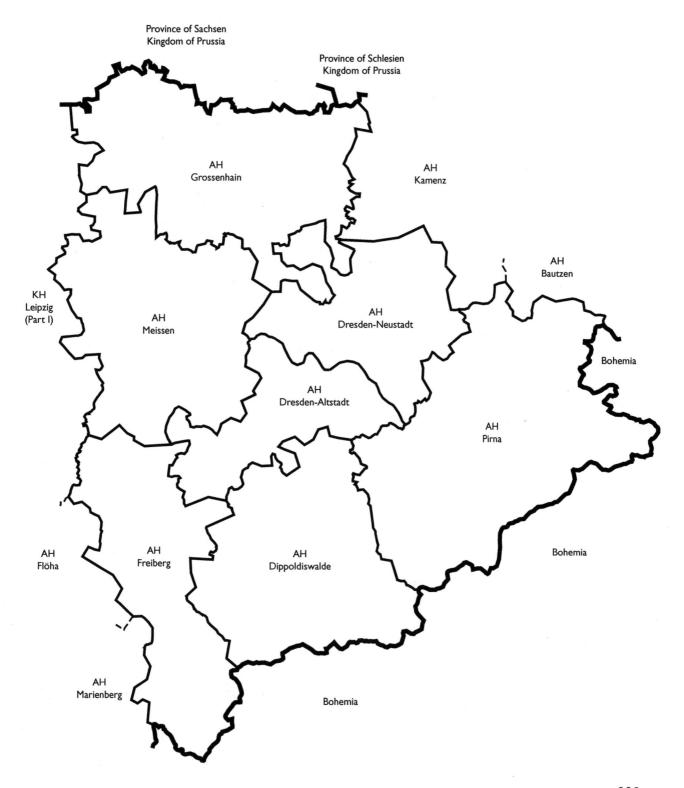

Province of Sachsen
Kingdom of Prussia

Province of Schlesien
Kingdom of Prussia

AH
Grossenhain

AH
Kamenz

AH
Bautzen

KH
Leipzig
(Part I)

AH
Meissen

AH
Dresden-Neustadt

Bohemia

AH
Dresden-Altstadt

AH
Pirna

AH
Flöha

AH
Freiberg

AH
Dippoldiswalde

Bohemia

AH
Marienberg

Bohemia

AMTSHAUPTMANNSCHAFT DIPPOLDISWALDE
CATHOLIC PARISHES

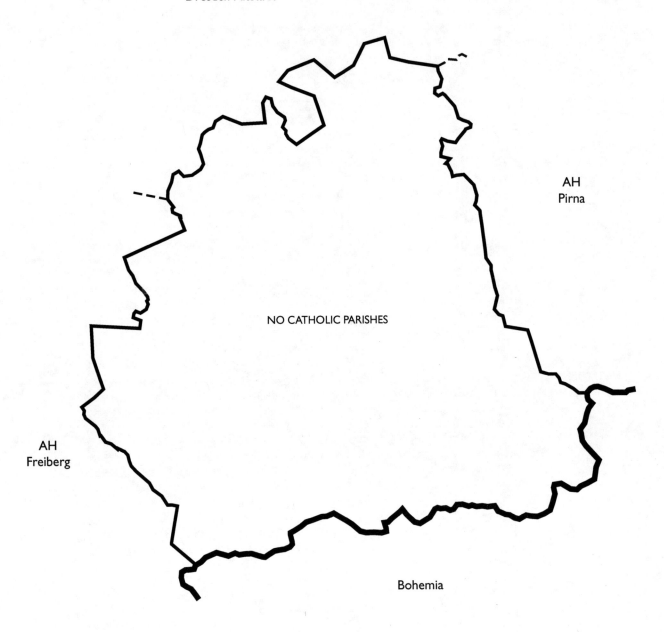

AH
Dresden-Altstadt

AH
Pirna

NO CATHOLIC PARISHES

AH
Freiberg

Bohemia

	10 miles		20 miles	
10 km		20 km	30 km	

TOWN KEY

Altenberg	Grossbörnchen	Niederjohnsbach..............
Altgeising	Grossölsa	Niederkreischa...............
Altgeorgenfeld	Hainichen.....................	Niedermalter ....
Ammelsdorf	Hänichen	Niederpöbel ....
Ammelsmühle...................	Hartmannsdorf................	Niederpretzschendorf ......
Babisnau......................	Hartmannsmühle	Niederreichstädt ....
Bärenburg.....................	Hennersdorf..................	Niederreinhardtsgrimma..
Bärenfels	Hermsdorf.....................	Obercunnersdorf.............
Bärenklau	Hirschbach...................	Oberfraundorf ....
Bärenklause..................	Hirschsprung	Oberhässlich.................
Bärenstein	Höckendorf	Oberhesslich.................
Beerwalde....................	Holzhau	Oberjohnsbach ....
Berrenth......................	Johnsbach	Oberkarsdorf.................
Bienenmühle...................	Kastamendörfel	Oberkreischa ....
Borlas	Kautzsch	Oberlöwenhain ....
Börnchen	Kipsdorf	Obermalter...................
Bröschen	Kleba	Obernaundorf ....
Bruchschenke.................	Kleinbobritzsch	Oberpretzschendorf........
Burkersdorf...................	Kleinbörnchen...............	Oberreichstädt ....
Cratzhammer.................	Kleincarsdorf.................	Oberreinhardtsgrimma.....
Cunnersdorf bei	Kleinhennersdorf	Obverpöbel ....
Reinhardtsgrimma	Kleinkarsdorf................	Panisdorf ....
Dippoldiswalda	Kleinkreischa	Panishain....................
Dippoldiswalde	Kratzhammer	Possendorf ....
Dittersbach	Kreischa.....................	Priessgen....................
Dittersdorf....................	Lauenstein...................	Prössgen ....
Dönischen....................	Liebenau	Quohren bei Kreischa......
Dönschten	Luchau......................	Rechenberg..................
Elend	Lungwitz	Rehefeld ....
Falkenhain	Malter.......................	Rehfeld ....
bei Schmiedeberg.......	Maltermühle.................	Reichenau ....
Frauenstein...................	Mittelkreischa................	Reichstädt...................
Friedersdorf..................	Müglitz	Reichstein...................
Fürstenau	Nassau	Reinberg ....
Fürstenwalde..................	Naundorf	Reinhardtsgrimma ....
Geising	bei Schmiedeberg.......	Rippien ....
Georgenfeld...................	Neubau	Röthenbach ....
Glashütte	Neudörfel bei Glashütte...	Rudolphsdorf ....
Gleisberg	Neugeising...................	Rückenhain..................
Gombsen	Neugeorgenfeld	Ruppendorf...................
Gottgetreu...................	Neuzinnwald	Sadisdorf ....
Gottreu......................	Niederjahnsbach.............	Saida ....

AMTSHAUPTMANNSCHAFT DRESDEN-ALTSTADT
CATHOLIC PARISHES

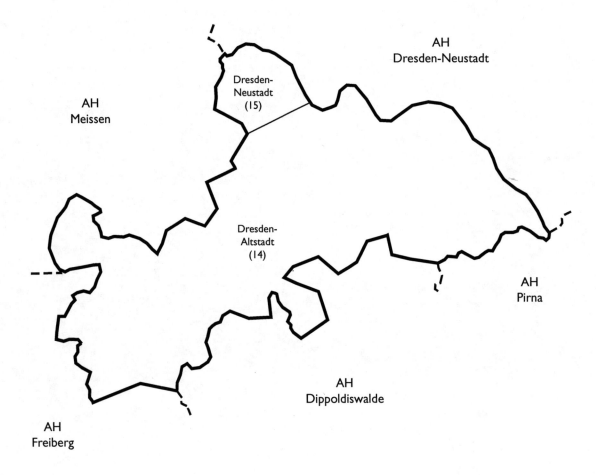

AH
Meissen

Dresden-
Neustadt
(15)

AH
Dresden-Neustadt

Dresden-
Altstadt
(14)

AH
Pirna

AH
Dippoldiswalde

AH
Freiberg

10 miles		20 miles	
10 km	20 km	30 km	

AMTSHAUPTMANNSCHAFT DRESDEN-NEUSTADT
CATHOLIC PARISHES

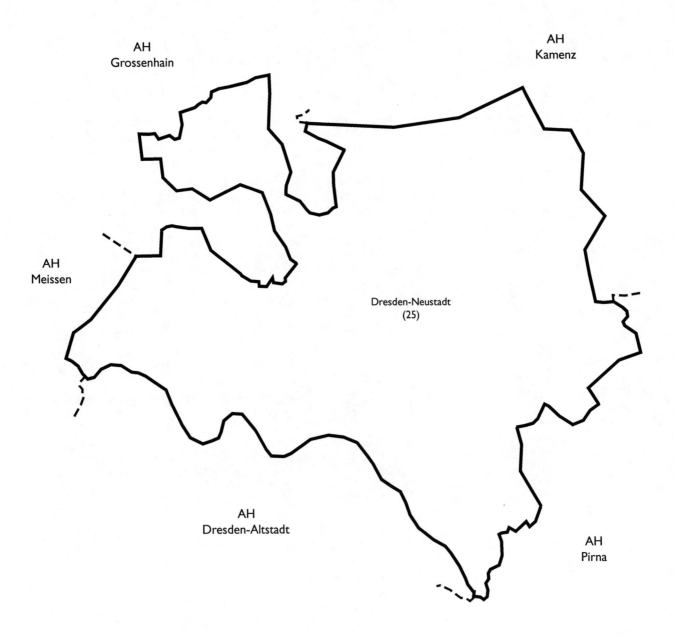

AH
Grossenhain

AH
Kamenz

AH
Meissen

Dresden-Neustadt
(25)

AH
Dresden-Altstadt

AH
Pirna

10 miles		20 miles	
10 km	20 km	30 km	

AMTSHAUPTMANNSCHAFT FREIBERG
CATHOLIC PARISHES

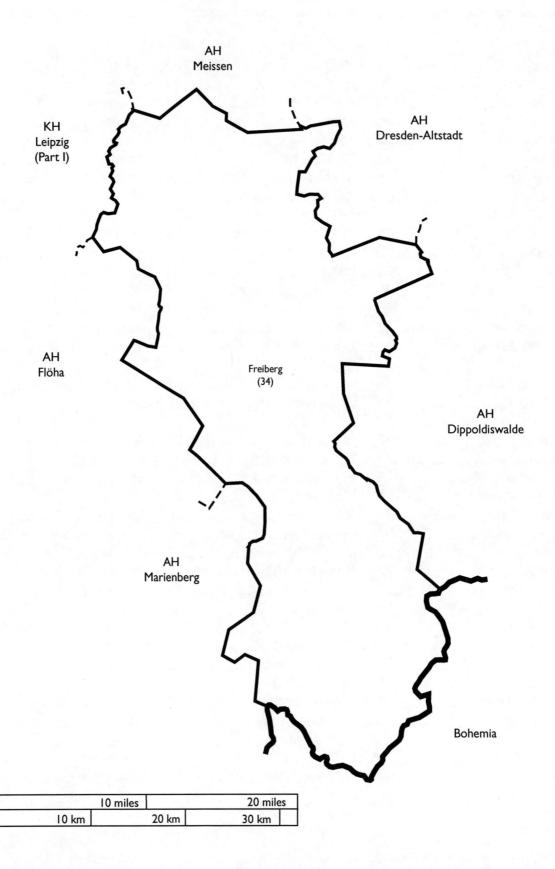

AH
Meissen

KH
Leipzig
(Part I)

AH
Dresden-Altstadt

AH
Flöha

Freiberg
(34)

AH
Dippoldiswalde

AH
Marienberg

Bohemia

10 miles		20 miles	
10 km	20 km	30 km	

AMTSHAUPTMANNSCHAFT GROSSENHAIN
CATHOLIC PARISHES

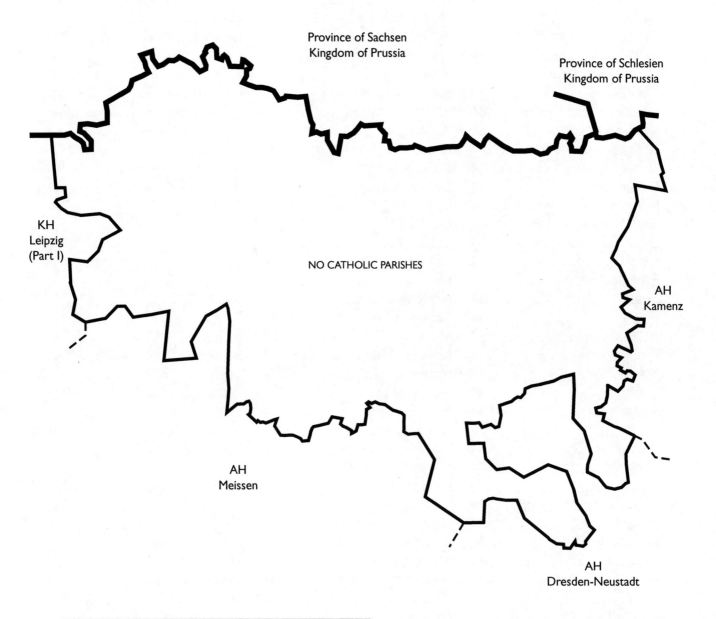

Province of Sachsen
Kingdom of Prussia

Province of Schlesien
Kingdom of Prussia

KH
Leipzig
(Part I)

NO CATHOLIC PARISHES

AH
Kamenz

AH
Meissen

AH
Dresden-Neustadt

	10 miles		20 miles	
10 km		20 km	30 km	

TOWN KEY

Adelsdorf	Gävernitz	Leckwitz..........................
Altleis	Geislitz...........................	Lenz................................
Altseusslitz.....................	Glaubitz	Leutewitz bei Riesa ....
Bärnsdorf.......................	Göhlis bei Riesa	Lichtensee ....
Basslitz	Göhra.............................	Liega..............................
bei Blattersleben........	Gohrisch	Linz................................
Basslitz bei Jessen	Golzscha.........................	Lorenzkirch ....
Bauda	Gorisch	Lorenzkirchen ....
Beiersdorf......................	Görzig	Lötzschen ....
Bernsdorf.......................	Grödel.............................	Lüttichau ....
Bieberach	Gröditz...........................	Lützschen ....
Blattersleben..................	Grossdittmannsdorf	Marksiedlitz.....................
Blochwitz	Grossenhain	Marsdorf ....
Boden	Grossraschütz	Medessen ....
Böhla bei Ortrandt	Grosszschepa..................	Medingen........................
Böhlau	Haidehäuser	Mergendorf ....
Borschütz.......................	Hain	Merschwitz......................
Briestewitz	Heide	Mershwitz ....
Brösnitz..........................	Heidehäuser	Milbitz ....
Cobenthal	Heyda bei Riesa	Mittelebersbach ....
Colmnitz.........................	Hohndorf.........................	Moritz..............................
Coselitz..........................	Jacobsthal	Mühlbach ....
Cosslitz..........................	Kalkreuth	Mülbitz ....
Cunertswalde..................	Kleindrebig......................	Nasseböhla......................
Cunnersdorf	Kleingeislitz.....................	Nauleis............................
an der Roder..............	Kleinraschütz..................	Naundorf bei Hain...........
Cunnertswalde................	Kleinthiermig...................	Naundorf bei Ortrandt......
Däbritzchen	Kleintrebnitz....................	Naundörfchen ....
Dallwitz	Kleinzschepa	Naunhof..........................
Debritzchen	Kmehlen	Nauwalde........................
Deschütz........................	Kobenthal	Neudorf...........................
Diesbar	Kolkwitz	Neuleis............................
Diesbsfehre	Koselitz	Neuseusslitz ....
Dobra.............................	Kottewitz an der Elbe......	Neusorge ....
Döbritzgen	Kottewitz bei Strauda.......	Niederebersbach ....
Döschütz........................	Krauschütz......................	Niederrödern....................
Ebersbach	Krausnitz.........................	Niederzschanitz...............
Erbmannsdorf.................	Kreinitz...........................	Niegerode ....
Ermendorf.......................	Lampertswalda	Nieska.............................
Folbern	Laubach..........................	Nüncheritz ....
Frauenhain	Lautendorf	Nünchritz ....
Freitelsdorf.....................	Lauterbach.......................	Oberebersbach................

AMTSHAUPTMANNSCHAFT MEISSEN
CATHOLIC PARISHES

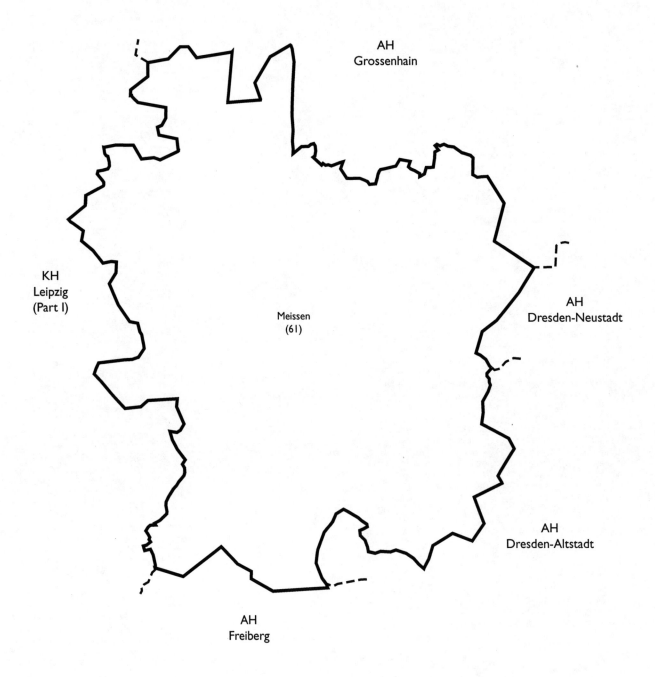

AH
Grossenhain

KH
Leipzig
(Part I)

Meissen
(61)

AH
Dresden-Neustadt

AH
Dresden-Altstadt

AH
Freiberg

10 miles		20 miles	
10 km	20 km	30 km	

PARISH KEY

61. Meissen...................... 1812911

TOWN KEY

347

AMTSHAUPTMANNSCHAFT PIRNA
CATHOLIC PARISHES

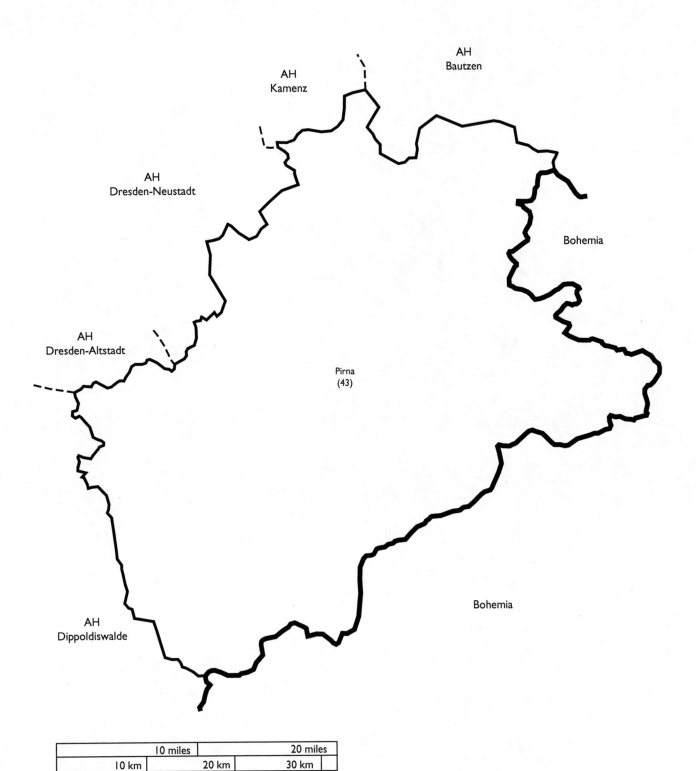

AH
Bautzen

AH
Kamenz

AH
Dresden-Neustadt

Bohemia

AH
Dresden-Altstadt

Pirna
(43)

AH
Dippoldiswalde

Bohemia

10 miles		20 miles	
10 km	20 km	30 km	

OTHER CHURCHES

Although the Lutheran and Catholic churches claim the largest percentage of the population in Germany, other denominations can be found throughout the country. The presence, availability, and concentration of these minority religions vary from one region of Germany to another. Jewish and Reformed Lutheran records are among those most frequently found although other religions are also represented. These minority religions are not always fully identified in the regional gazetteers making it difficult to determine which are available for each region. The following list identifies some of the minority religions in the Kingdom of Saxony, although there may be other congregations not shown due to missing, inadequate, or difficult to decipher information in the gazetteers. In most instances the specific congregation or one of the regional archives can be contacted for each area.

JEWISH RECORDS

The local Jewish communities in Germany are represented by the Zentralrat der Juden in Deutschland with a regional federation office located in Bonn.

Zentralrat der Juden in Deutschland
Rungsdorferstrasse 6
5300 Bonn 2
Website: http://www.zentralratdjuden.de/en/topic/2.html

Landsverband Sachsen der Jüdischen Gemeinden
Hasenberg 1
01067 Dresden

Dresden 1184471
Annaberg 1184462

TOWN INDEX

TOWN	LUTHERAN	CATHOLIC	TOWN	LUTHERAN	CATHOLIC
A			Amtsstruppen	289	353
			Annaberg	241	315
Abend	283	347	Ansprung	255	323
Abtei-Oberlungwitz	259	327	Antonstadt	267	335
Adelsdorf	279	343	Arnsdorf	223	297
Albersdorf	245	317		271	339
Albertitz	283	347	Arnsfeld	241	315
Alberts-Rachlau	223	297	Arntitz	283	347
Alberts-Rackel	223	297	au dem Wehricht	251	321
Albertsthal	251	321	Auerbach	259	327
Albrechtsdorf	237	311	Auerhaus	271	339
Aldorf	245	317	Auerswalde	247	319
Alt Bernsdorf	233	307	Augusttusthal	237	311
Altchemnitz	245	317	Augustusbad	271	339
Alt Choren	283	347	Augustusberg	283	347
Altcoschütz	267	335	Augustusburg	247	319
Altcunnewitz	233	307	Auritz	223	297
Altdresden	267	335	Auschkowitz	229	303
Alteibau	233	307	Äusserst Sohland	223	297
Altenberg	263	331			
Altendorf	245	317	**B**		
	289	353			
Altenhain	229	303	Baademühle	255	323
	247	319	Babisnau	263	331
Alte Ziegelscheune	229	303	Badersen	283	347
Altfranken	267	335	Bahra	283	347
Altgeising	263	331	Bannewitz	267	335
Altgeorgenfeld	263	331	Bärenburg	263	331
Altgersdorf	237	311	Bärenfels	263	331
Alt Hirschstein	283	347	Bärenhau	289	353
Althöfchen	283	347	Bärenklau	263	331
Althöffchen	283	347	Bärenklause	263	331
Alt Hörnitz	237	311	Bärenlohe	241	315
Altjohnsdorf	237	311	Bärenstein	241	315
Altjonsdorf	237	311		263	331
Altkaitz	267	335	Barmitz	284	347
Altklingenberg	267	335	Barnitz	284	347
Altleis	279	343	Bärnsdorf	279	343
Alt Lommatzsch	283	347	Barosche	223	297
Altrobschütz	283	347	Baruth	223	297
Altsattel	283	347	Bärwalda	271	339
Altscheibe	237	311	Basankwitz	223	297
Altscheidenbach	223	297	Baschütz	223	297
Altseusslitz	279	343	Basslitz		
Altstadt	237	311	bei Blattersleben	279	343
	267	335	Basslitz bei Jessen	279	343
	289	353	Bauda	279	343
Altstadt-Waldenburg	251	321	Baudissin	223	297
Alttanneberg	283	347	Baudorf	284	347
Alt-Waldenburg	251	321	Bautzen	223	297
Altwaltersdorf	237	311	Bautzin	223	297
Alt Zaschendorf	283	347	Bederwitz	223	297
Ammelsdorf	263	331	Beerwalde	263	331
Ammelsmühle	263	331	Beicha	284	347
			Beiermühle	284	347

TOWN	LUTHERAN	CATHOLIC	TOWN	LUTHERAN	CATHOLIC
Beiersdorf	279	343	Birkau	223	297
Beiersdorf			Birkenhain	284	347
bei Neusalza	233	307	Birkenroda	223	297
Beisorge	247	319	Birkigt	267	335
Belbitz	233	307	Birkwitz	289	353
Belgern	223	297	Birmenitz	284	347
Bellschwitz	223	297	Bischdorf	233	307
Bellwitz	233	307	Bischheim	229	303
Belmsdorf	223	297	Bischofswerda	223	297
Belzmühle	245	317	Blankenstein	284	347
Berba	284	347	Blattersleben	279	343
Berbisdorf	245	317	Blauer Stern	233	307
	271	339	Bloaschütz	223	297
Berenbach	229	303	Blochwitz	279	343
Berge	223	297	Blösa	223	297
Berggieshübel	289	353	Blumberg	237	311
Berggut	241	315	Blumenau	255	323
Berghäusel	241	315	Blumenhof	241	315
Berghäuser	284	347	Bobershau	255	323
Berghäuser bei Stolpen	289	353	Boblitz	223	297
Bergmühle	284	347	Bocka	229	303
Bergwerk	284	347	Bocka bei Luppa	223	297
Bernbruch	229	303	Bockau	255	323
Bernsdorf	245	317	Bocken	284	347
	247	319	Bockwein	284	347
	251	321	Bockwen	284	347
	279	343	Bockwitz	284	347
Bernshäuser	284	347	Boden	279	343
Bernstadt			Bodenbach	284	347
auf dem Eigen	233	307	Boden		
Bernstein	251	321	mit Schindelbach	255	323
Berntitz bei Staucha	284	347	Bodenmühle	255	323
Berrenth	263	331	Boderitz	229	303
Berthelsdorf	233	307		267	335
	251	321	Bodnitz	267	335
	275	341	Bogatynia	238	312
	289	353	Böhla	284	347
Bertsdorf	237	311	Böhla bei Ortrandt	279	343
Berzdorf	233	307	Böhlau	279	343
Berzdorf			Böhlen	284	347
auf dem Eigen	233	307	Böhmisch	229	303
Beutig	284	347	Böhmisch Bollung	229	303
Białopole	238	312	Böhmische Folge	229	303
Bieberach	279	343	Bohnitzsch	284	347
Bieberstein	284	347	Bohra	229	303
Biedrzychowice Górne	237	311	Bolbritz	223	297
Biehla	229	303	Bonnewitz	289	353
	271	339	Boritz	284	347
	289	353	Borlas	263	331
Bienenmühle	263	331	Borna	245	317
Bienhof	289	353		289	353
Biensdorf	247	319	Bornau	245	317
	289	353	Börnchen	247	319
Binnewitz	223	297		263	331

TOWN	LUTHERAN	CATHOLIC	TOWN	LUTHERAN	CATHOLIC
Börnersdorf	289	353	Brösnitz	279	343
Börnichen			Bruchschenke	263	331
bei Oederan	247	319	Brückengut	247	319
Börnichen			Brüderwiese	275	341
bei Zschorau	247	319	Brünlos	259	327
Bornitz	223	297	Brünnlastgüter	241	315
Bornitz			Buchholz	241	315
bei Lommatzsch	284	347		271	339
Borsberg	271	339	Buchholz bei Bocka	223	297
Borschütz	279	343	Buchwald	241	315
Borstendorf	247	319	Buchwalda	223	297
Borthen	289	353	Buda	233	307
Bosewitz	289	353	Bühlau	271	339
Bottendorfer Mühle	241	315		289	353
Boxdorf	271	339	Bulleritz	229	303
Boxdorfer			Burgstädtel	241	315
Weinsbergflur	271	339	Burgstädtel bei Borthen	289	353
Brabschütz	267	335	Burgstädtel		
Brand	275	341	bei Briessnitz	267	335
Bratków	237	311	Burk	223	297
Brauna	229	303	Bürkau	223	297
Braunsdorf	247	319	Burkersdorf	237	311
Bräunsdorf	245	317		245	317
	247	319		263	331
	275	341		284	347
Braunsdorf			Burkhardswalde	289	353
bei Tharandt	284	347	Burkhardtsdorf	245	317
Brauschwitz	229	303	Burkhardtswalde	284	347
Brausenstein	289	353	Buscheritz	223	297
Brautitz	229	303	Buschermühle	223	297
Brechhaus	255	323	Buschmühle	237	311
Brehmen	223	297		241	315
Breiteberg	237	311		284	347
Breite Lehn	245	317	Buschschenke	229	303
Breitenau	247	319	Buschvorwerk	237	311
	289	353	Butterberg	237	311
Breitenbach	251	321	Buttervorwerk	237	311
	284	347			
Breitenberg	284	347	**C**		
Breitendorf	233	307			
Breske	223	297	Calinberg	251	321
Bretnig	229	303	Callenberg	223	297
Brettnig	223	297		251	321
Briesing	223	297	Camenz	229	303
Briesnitz	267	335	Caminau		
Briessnitz	223	297	bei Königswartha	223	297
Briestewitz	279	343	Caminau bei Radibor	223	297
Brockwitz	284	347	Cammerhof	289	353
Brohna	223	297	Cämmerswalde	275	341
Brösa	223	297	Canitz bei Meissen	284	347
Brösang	223	297	Canitz Christina	223	297
Bröschen	263	331	Cannewitz	223	297
Broschwitz	284	347	Cannewitz bei Gröditz	223	297
Brosen	284	347			

TOWN	LUTHERAN	CATHOLIC	TOWN	LUTHERAN	CATHOLIC
Cannewitz			Cunewalde	233	307
bei Marienstern	229	303	Cunnersdorf	241	315
Carlsberg	223	297		247	319
Carlsbrunn	233	307	Cunnersdorf		
Carlsdorf	223	297	an der Roder	279	343
Carlsruhe	223	297	Cunnersdorf		
Caseritz	229	303	auf dem Eigen	233	307
Casslau	223	297	Cunnersdorf		
Catharinenberg	275	341	bei Helfenberg	271	339
Cauritz	251	321	Cunnersdorf		
Charlottenruh	237	311	bei Hohnstein	289	353
Chemnitz	245	317	Cunnersdorf bei Kaitz	267	335
Churschütz	284	347	Cunnersdorf		
Classenbach	245	317	bei Kamenz	229	303
Clausnitz	275	341	Cunnersdorf		
Clieben	284	347	bei Königstein	289	353
Closter Freiheit	237	311	Cunnersdorf bei Lausa	271	339
Clostermühle	245	317	Cunnersdorf bei Pirna	289	353
	284	347	Cunnersdorf bei		
Cobenthal	279	343	Reinhardtsgrimma	263	331
Coblenz	223	297	Cunnertswalde	279	343
Cölln	223	297	Cunnewitz		
	284	347	bei Marienstern	229	303
Colmnitz	279	343		233	307
Commerau bei Kauppa	223	297			
Commerau			**D**		
bei Königswartha	223	297	Däbritzchen	279	343
Conradsdorf	275	341	Dahlowitz	223	297
Constappel	284	347	Dahnwiese		
Copitz	289	353	bei Dresden	271	339
Cortnitz	223	297	Dahren	223	297
Coschütz	267	335	Dallwitz	280	343
Cosel bei Königsbrück	229	303	Dammmühle	247	319
Cosel im Gebirge	223	297		255	323
Coselitz	279	343	Daranitz	223	297
Cossern	223	297	das Rothe Gut	284	347
Cosslitz	279	343	das Rothe Haus	255	323
Cosswiger				284	347
Weinbergsgemeinde	284	347	das Rothe Vorwerk	241	315
Coswig	284	347		245	317
Cotta	267	335		275	341
Cranzahl	241	315	das Weise Vorwerk	241	315
Cränzmühle	233	307	das Weisse Gut	241	315
Cratza	289	353	Daube	289	353
Cratzhammer	263	331	Daubermühle	289	353
Crostau	223	297	Daubnitz	284	347
Crostwitz	229	303	Debritzchen	280	343
Crotenlaide	251	321	Deila	284	347
Crotta	289	353	Deltzschen	267	335
Crottendorf	241	315	Demitz	223	297
Crumhermsdorf	289	353	Denkwitz	223	297
Crummenhennersdorf	275	341	Dennheritz	251	321
Cunersdorf	241	315	Dennschütz	284	347
Cunertswalde	279	343			

TOWN	LUTHERAN	CATHOLIC	TOWN	LUTHERAN	CATHOLIC
der blaue Stern	233	307	Doberzeit	289	353
der niedere Zug	275	341	Dobisch	284	347
der obere Zug	275	341	Dobra	280	343
der Raum	241	315		289	353
der Rothe Pfütze	255	323	Döbra	229	303
der Weisse Hirsch	255	323		289	353
	271	339	Dobranitz	224	297
der Wilde Mann	289	353	Dobrig	229	303
Deschütz	280	343	Dobritz	284	347
Deuben	267	335	Döbritzgen	280	343
Deutsch Baselitz	229	303	Döbschke	224	297
Deutschcatharinenberg	275	341	Dobschütz	284	347
Deutscheinsiedel	275	341	Döhlen bei Bautzen	224	297
Deutschenbohra	284	347	Döhlen bei Dresden	267	335
Deutschenbora	284	347	Dohma	271	339
Deutschgeorgenthal	275	341	Dohna	289	353
Deutschneudorf	275	341	Doigowitz	233	307
Diehmen	223	297	Döltzschen	267	335
Diensdorf	271	339	Domselwitz	284	347
Diera	284	347	Dönischen	263	331
die Rothe Mühle	229	303	Dönschten	263	331
	241	315	Dorfchemnitz	259	327
	284	347	Dorfchemnitz		
Diesbar	280	343	bei Sayda	275	341
Diesbsfehre	280	343	Dörfel	237	311
Dietrich	251	321		241	315
Dippelsdorf	271	339		255	323
Dippoldiswalda	263	331	Dorfmehlen	289	353
Dippoldiswalde	263	331	Dorfmühle	241	315
Dirnhof			Dorfschellenberg	247	319
bei Berggieshübel	289	353	Dornhennersdorf	237	311
Dittelsdorf	237	311	Dornhof	289	353
Dittersbach	247	319	Dörnthal	275	341
	263	331	Dorotheenberg	245	317
	275	341	Dörschnitz	284	347
	289	353	Döschütz	280	343
Dittersbach			Dösig	284	347
auf dem Eigen	233	307	Dösitz	284	347
Dittersbacher			Drachenwald	255	323
Wiesenhäuser	289	353	Draisdorf	245	317
Dittersdorf	247	319	Drauschkowitz	224	297
	259	327	Drauschwitz	233	307
	263	331	Draussendorf	237	311
Dittmannsdorf	247	319	Drebach	255	323
	284	347	Drehbach	255	323
Dittmannsdorf			Drehfeld	284	347
bei Sayda	275	341	Drehsa	224	297
Dittrich	251	321	Dreikretscham	224	297
Döberkütz	223	297	Dreissig	284	347
Doberschau	224	297	Dreiwerden	247	319
Doberschütz			Dresden-Alstadt	267	335
bei Neschwitz	224	297	Dresden-Neustadt	271	339
Doberschütz			Dretschen	224	297
bei Niedergurig	224	297	Droben	224	297

TOWN	LUTHERAN	CATHOLIC	TOWN	LUTHERAN	CATHOLIC
Drossel	284	347	Erdmannsdorf	247	319
Dubranke	224	297	Erfenschlag	245	317
Dubrau	224	297	Erlbach	259	327
Dürre Bühlau	271	339	Erlicht	275	341
Dürre Fuchs	289	353	Erlichtgut	284	347
Dürrenuhlsdorf	251	321	Erlichtmühle bei Elstra	229	303
Dürrhennersdorf	233	307		290	353
Dürrhof	289	353	Ermendorf	280	343
Dürr Jessnitz	224	297	Ernstthal	251	321
Dürrröhrsdorf	289	353	Errlicht	275	341
Dürrwicknitz	229	303	Eschdorf	290	353
Dzialoszyn	237	311	Eschenbach		
			bei Wolkenstein	255	323
E			Euba	245	317
			Eubenberg	245	317
Ebendörfel	224	297	Euldorf	233	307
Ebenheit bei Pirne	289	353	Eule	271	339
Ebenheit unterm			Eulenmühle	284	347
Lilienstein	289	353	Eulitz	284	347
Ebersbach	233	307	Eulmühle	290	353
	247	319	Eulowitz	224	297
	251	321	Eutrich	224	297
	280	343	Eutschütz	267	335
Ebersdorf	233	307			
	247	319	**F**		
Eckartsberg	237	311			
	284	347	Falken	251	321
Eckersberg	237	311	Falkenau	247	319
Eckersdorf	267	335	Falkenbach	255	323
Ehrenberg	290	353	Falkenberg	224	297
Ehrenfriedersdorf	241	315		275	341
Eibenberg	245	317	Falkenhain bei Dohna	290	353
Eichgraben	237	311	Falkenhain		
Eichlaide	251	321	bei Schmiedeberg	263	331
Eichtermühle	224	297	Falkenhäuser	224	297
Einsiedel	245	317	Feldhaus	237	311
	275	341	Feldhäuser	233	307
Einsiedel-	255	323	Feldleuba	237	311
Eisenberg	271	339	Feldschönau	233	307
Eiserode auf dem Eigen	233	307	Fernrückerswalde	255	323
Eisschenke	290	353	Fichte	290	353
Elbe	290	353	Fichtelschenke	233	307
Elbersdorf	290	353	Finkenburg	247	319
Elend	263	331	Finsterau	241	315
Elgersdorf	284	347	Fischbach	290	353
Ellersdorf	224	297	Fischergasse		
Elstra	229	303	bei Meissen	284	347
Elterlein	241	315	Fischhaus	247	319
Elzenberg	251	321		255	323
Engelmühle	251	321	Fleissig	224	297
Entenschenke	224	297	Flöha	247	319
Eppendorf	247	319	Flosslohnhaus		
Erbisdorf	275	341	bei Görsdorf	255	323
Erbmannsdorf	280	343	Flossmühle	247	319

TOWN	LUTHERAN	CATHOLIC	TOWN	LUTHERAN	CATHOLIC
Folbern	280	343	Garnsdorf	247	319
Fördergersdorf	267	335	Garsebach	284	347
Förderjessen	290	353	Gärtitz	284	347
Förstel	241	315	Gasern	284	347
Forsthaus Grünthal	255	323	Gässnitz	251	321
Forsthaus Heidelbach	255	323	Gaussig	224	297
Forsthaus Kriegwald	241	315	Gaustritz	267	335
Forstmühle	229	303	Gávernitz	284	347
Franken	251	321	Gävernitz	280	343
Frankenberg	247	319	Gebirge	255	323
Frankenhof	251	321	Geiersberg	241	315
Frankenstein	247	319	Geiersdorf	241	315
Frankenthal	224	297	Geising	263	331
Frauenbach	275	341	Geislitz	280	343
Frauenhain	280	343	Geisslitz	224	297
Frauenstein	263	331	Geissmannsdorf	224	297
Fraunbach	275	341	Gelenau	229	303
Freiberg	275	341		241	315
Freibergsdorf	275	341	Gelobtes Land	255	323
Freihufe zu Neukirch	229	303	Georgenfeld	263	331
Freikäuser	224	297	Georgewitz	233	307
Freitelsdorf	280	343	Geppersdorf	290	353
Friedebach	275	341	Gerinswalde	255	323
Friedeburg	275	341	Gersdorf	255	323
Friedelmühle	241	315		290	353
Friedensthal	233	307	Gertitzsch	284	347
Friedersdorf	229	303	Gesau	251	321
	263	331	Geyer	241	315
	271	339	Gickelshäuser	224	297
Friedersdorf			Giedlitz	224	297
bei Reibersdorf	237	311	Giessenstein	290	353
Friedreich	237	311	Giessmannsdorf	237	311
Friedrich	237	311	Glashütte	263	331
Friedrichstadt	267	335	Glaubitz	280	343
Friedrichstal	271	339	Glaubnitz	229	303
Friedrichswalde	290	353	Glauchau	251	321
Fritzkau	233	307	Glauschnitz	229	303
Frohnau	241	315	Gleina	224	297
Fürstenau	263	331		284	347
Fürstenhain	271	339	Gleisberg	263	331
Fürstenthal	275	341	Glösa	245	317
Fürstenwalde	263	331	Glossen	233	307
Furth	245	317	Gnaschwitz	224	297
			Göbeln	224	297
G			Göda	224	297
			Gödelitz	284	347
Gabel	271	339	Gödlau	229	303
Gablenz	245	317	Goes	290	353
	259	327	Goess	290	353
Gahlenz	247	319	Gohla	284	347
Galgenschenke	224	297	Göhlenau	229	303
Gallschutz	284	347	Gohlis	284	347
Gamig	290	353	Göhlis	284	347
Ganernitz	284	347	Göhlis bei Riesa	280	343

TOWN	LUTHERAN	CATHOLIC	TOWN	LUTHERAN	CATHOLIC
Göhra	280	343	Griesbachmühle	255	323
Gohrisch	280	343	Griessbach	255	323
	290	353	Grillenburg	267	335
Göhrisch	284	347	Gröbern	284	347
Golberode	267	335	Grödel	280	343
Goldbach	224	297	Gröditz	224	297
Goldgrund	284	347		280	343
Golk	284	347	Groitzsch	290	353
Göltsche	284	347	Grossbörnchen	263	331
Golzscha	280	343	Grossborthen	290	353
Gölzscha	284	347	Grossbröhsern	224	297
Gombsen	263	331	Grossbrösern	224	297
Gomlitz	271	339	Grossburgk	267	335
Gommern	290	353	Grosscotta	290	353
Gommlitz	271	339	Grossdehsa	233	307
Gompitz	267	335	Grossdittmannsdorf	280	343
Gönnsdorf	271	339	Grossdobritz	284	347
Gönsdorf	271	339	Grossdöbschütz	224	297
Goppeln	267	335	Grossdorfhain	267	335
Göppersdorf	290	353	Grossdrebnitz	224	297
Görbersdorf	247	319	Grossdubrau	224	298
Gorisch	280	343	Grossenhain	280	343
	290	353	Grosserkmannsdorf	271	339
Gorknitz	290	353	Grossförstchen	224	298
Görna	284	347	Grossgaussig	224	298
Gornau	247	319	Grossgrabe	229	303
Gornsdorf	259	327	Grossgraupe	271	339
Görsdorf	255	323	Grosshähnchen	224	298
Görtitz	284	347	Grossharthau	290	353
Gorusdorf	259	327	Grosshartmannsdorf	275	341
Görzig	280	343	Grosshennersdorf	233	307
Gościszów	237	311	Grossjahna	284	347
Gosdorf	290	353	Grosskagen	284	347
Gossdorf	290	353	Grosskunitz	224	298
Gosswitz	233	307	Grossluga	290	353
Gostewitz	284	347	Grossnaundorf	271	339
Gostritz	267	335	Grossockrilla	271	339
Gottgetreu	263	331	Grossolbersdorf	255	323
Gotthelffriedrichsgrund	284	347	Grossölsa	263	331
Gottleuba	290	353	Grossopitz	267	335
Gottreu	263	331	Grossporitzsch	237	311
Gottschdorf	229	303	Grosspostwitz	224	298
Grabischau	284	347	Grossprausitz	284	347
Grabisch Mühle	284	347	Grosspresen	224	298
Grafenhofschenke	224	297	Grossraschütz	280	343
	284	347	Grossröhrsdorf	229	303
Gränitz	275	341	Grossröhrsdorf		
Gränze	229	303	bei Pirna	284	347
Gränzmühle	251	321	Grossröhrsdorf		
Graupzig	284	347	bei Radeberg	229	303
Grauschütz	284	347	Grossrückerswalde	255	323
Grebern	284	347	Grossrümpf	251	321
Greenfield	251	321	Grossschirma	275	341
Griesbach	255	323	Grossschönau	237	311

TOWN	LUTHERAN	CATHOLIC	TOWN	LUTHERAN	CATHOLIC
Grossschweidnitz	233	307	Hahnmühle	229	303
Grosssedlitz	290	353	Haidehäuser	280	343
Grossseitschen	224	298	Hain	237	311
Grosstrebnitz	233	307		280	343
Grossvoigtsberg	275	341	Haine	233	307
Grosswaltersdorf	247	319	Hainersdorf	290	353
Grosswelka	224	298	Hainewalde	237	311
Grosswüstalbertitz	284	347	Haingut	255	323
Grosszschachwitz	290	353	Hainichen	263	331
Grosszschepa	280	343	Hainitz	224	298
Grötzsch	284	347	Hainsbach	267	335
Grubditz	224	298	Hainsberg	267	335
Grube	233	307	Hainzbauk	255	323
Gruben	284	347	Halbau	233	307
Grubschütz	224	298	Halbe	234	307
Grüllenburg	267	335	Halbendorf	237	311
Grüllenburger	267	335	Halbendorf		
Grumbach	241	315	an der Spree	224	298
	251	321	Halbendorf im Gebirge	224	298
	284	347	Halbestadt	290	353
Grüna	245	317	Hallbach	275	341
Gruna bei Nossen	284	347	Hals	275	341
Grunau	237	311	Halsbach	275	341
Grünau	255	323	Halsbrücke	275	341
Grünaue	284	347	Hamburg	267	335
Grünberg	229	303	Hammer-	241	315
	247	319	Hammermühle	241	315
	271	339		247	319
Grünbusch	224	298	Hammerunter-		
Grund	267	335	wiesenthal	241	315
Grundau	255	323	Hänichen	263	331
Grundhäuser	267	335	Hannitz	224	298
Grundmühle	241	315	Hartha	247	319
	290	353		267	335
Grüne Tanne	267	335		284	347
Grünfeld	251	321	Harthau	237	311
Grüngräbchen	229	303		245	317
Grünhainichen	247	319		251	321
Grünthal	255	323		290	353
Grützemühle	245	317	Hartmannsdorf	263	331
Gückelsberg	247	319	Hartmannsmühle	263	331
Guhra	224	298	Haselbacher Mühle	259	327
Gunnersdorf	247	319	Haselberg	290	353
Günsdorf	259	327	Haseldorf	229	303
Günthersdorf	224	298	Häselicht	290	353
Gutta	224	298	Hasenberg	237	311
Guttamelda	224	298	Hasenbrücke	275	341
Guttau	224	298	Hässlich	229	303
Güttersee	267	335	Haublermühle	251	321
			Haubolds Pulvermühle		
H			bei Olbernhau	255	323
			Hausberg	290	353
Haberdörfel	224	298			
Hahngut	255	323			

TOWN	LUTHERAN	CATHOLIC	TOWN	LUTHERAN	CATHOLIC
Hausdorf	229	303	Hertigswalde	290	353
	247	319	Herwigsdorf bei Löbau	234	307
	290	353	Herzogswalde	284	348
Häuser am Kühberg	241	315	Hessdorf	247	319
Häuser am Mühlberg	284	348	Hetzdorf	275	341
Häuser am Plossen	284	348	Hetzwalde	237	311
Häuser am Rauenthal	284	348	Heyda bei Riesa	280	343
Häuslermühle	251	321	Heynersdorf	245	317
Haussdorf	290	353	Hilbersdorf	245	317
Hauswalde	229	303		275	341
Haynewalde	237	311	Hilmersdorf	255	323
Heeselicht	290	353	Himmelmühle	255	323
Heeselichtmühle	290	353	Hintercossebaude	267	335
Heickendorf	251	321	Hintergersdorf	267	335
Heida	280	343	Hinterhermsdorf	290	353
Heide	280	343	Hinterjessen	290	353
Heidehäuser	280	343	Hintermauer	284	348
Heidelbach	275	341	Hintermühle	247	319
Heidelberg	275	341	Hinterottendorf	290	353
Heidenau	290	353	Hirschbach	263	331
Heidersdorf	275	341	Hirschberg	255	323
Heiersdorf	247	319	Hirschfeld	284	348
	251	321	Hirschfelde	237	311
Heilsberg	267	335	Hirschgrundmühle	259	327
Heinersdorf	245	317	Hirschleitmühle	255	323
Heinitz	284	348	Hirschmühle	290	353
Heinzebank	255	323	Hirschsprung	263	331
Heinzwaldmühle	255	323	Hirschstein	255	323
Helbersdorf	245	317	Hochkirch	234	307
Helbigsdorf	284	348	Höckendorf	229	303
Helfenberg	271	339		251	321
Hellendorf	290	353		263	331
Helmsdorf	290	353	Hofehäuser	271	339
Hempel	234	307	Höfgen	229	303
Hennersbach	290	353	Hofhainersdorf	290	353
Hennersdorf	247	319	Höflein	229	303
	263	331	Hoflösnitz	271	339
	290	353	Hohburkersdorf	290	353
Hennersdorf			Hohe Fichte	247	319
bei Kamenz	229	303	Hohe Linde	247	319
Hennitz	284	348	Hoheneck	259	327
Henschenne	234	307	Hohenfichte	247	319
Herbergen	290	353	Hohenlinde	247	319
Hermsdorf	251	321	Hohenstein	251	321
	263	331	Hohentanne	284	348
	271	339	Hohkirch	234	307
Hermsdorf			Hohndorf	251	321
bei Königstein	290	353		255	323
Herold	255	323		280	343
Herrenwalde	237	311	Hohngut	241	315
Herrmannsdorf	241	315	Hohnstein	290	353
Herrndorf	275	341	Höllenguth	290	353
Herrnhut	234	307	Höllenmühle	247	319
Herrnmühle	259	327	Hollscha	224	298

TOWN	LUTHERAN	CATHOLIC	TOWN	LUTHERAN	CATHOLIC
Holsch Dubrau	224	298	Jetschoba	224	298
Holzecke	284	348	Jiedlitz	229	303
Hölzelmühle	255	323	Joachimstein	234	307
Holzhau	263	331	Jocuschberg	284	348
Holzhäuser	251	321	Johannishof	290	353
Hopfgarten	255	323	Johannisthal	290	353
Horka	229	303	Johnsbach	263	331
Hormersdorf	259	327	Johnsdorf	224	298
Hosterwitz	271	339		237	311
Hübelschenke	224	298	Jöhstadt	241	315
Hühndorf	284	348	Jokischberg	284	348
Hünerkopf	241	315	Josephidorf	237	311
Huth	255	323	Josephsdorf	237	311
Hutha	275	341	Juchheh	267	335
Huthe	275	341	Jüdenberg	284	348
Hütten	284	348	Jüdenhain	251	321
Hütten bei Königstein	290	353		255	323
Hüttengrund	255	323			
Hüttengrundmühle	255	323	**K**		
Hüttenmühle	251	321			
			Kaditz	271	339
I			Kaditzäbschütz	284	348
			Kaisitz	284	348
Ibanitz	284	348	Kaitz	267	335
Ickowitz	284	348	Kalkreuth	234	307
Ilkendorf	284	348		280	343
Irbersdorf	247	319	Kamenz	229	303
Irgersdorf	224	298	Kändler	245	317
			Kanitz	284	348
J			Kappel	245	317
			Kappelmühle	241	315
Jacobsthal	280	343	Karcha	284	348
Jädenhain	255	323	Karnmühle	255	323
Jägerhof	247	319	Karrenmühle		
Jahnishausen	284	348	bei Rittersberg	255	323
Jahnsbach	241	315	Kaschka	285	348
Jahnsdorf	259	327	Kaschwitz	229	303
Jähsnitz	251	321	Käseberg	285	348
Jänkowitz	224	298	Kastamendörfel	263	331
Jannowitz	224	298	Käthewitz	285	348
Jäschütz	224	298	Katschwitz	224	298
Jasna Góra	238	311	Katzenberg	285	348
Jauer	229	303	Katzenhäuser	285	348
Jauernick	234	307	Kaufbach	285	348
Jenkwitz	224	298	Kauppa	224	298
Jensdorf	224	298	Kauscha	267	335
Jerisau	251	321	Kautzsch	263	331
Jesau	229	303	Keilbusch	285	348
Jeschütz	224	298	Keilbuschhäuser	285	348
Jessen bei Lommatzsch	284	348	Kemnitz	234	307
Jessen bei Okrilla	284	348		267	335
Jesseritz	284	348	Kemptau	245	317
Jessnitz	224	298	Kerbisdorf	234	307
Jessritz	284	348	Kertzsch	251	321
Jetscheba	224	298			

TOWN	LUTHERAN	CATHOLIC	TOWN	LUTHERAN	CATHOLIC
Kesselsdorf	224	298	Kleinhennersdorf	264	331
	285	348		290	353
Kettewitz	285	348	Kleinjänkowitz	224	298
Ketzergasse	285	348	Kleinkagen	285	348
Kiebnitz	234	307	Kleinkarsdorf	264	331
Kieschau	224	298	Kleinkreischa	264	331
Kiesdorf auf dem Eigen	234	307	Kleinkunitz	224	298
Kindisch	224	298	Kleinleichnam	224	298
	229	303	Kleinlimbach	245	317
Kipsdorf	263	331	Kleinluga	290	353
Kirchbach	247	319	Kleinnaundorf	267	335
Kirchberg	259	327	Kleinneuschönberg	275	341
Kittlitz	234	307	Kleinockrilla	271	339
Klappendorf	285	348	Kleinolbersdorf	245	317
Klappermühle	241	315	Kleinölsa	267	335
Klatenstein	237	311	Kleinopitz	285	348
Klatzschmühle	255	323	Kleinpestitz	267	335
Kleba	263	331	Kleinporitzsch	237	311
Kleebusch	224	298	Kleinpostwitz	224	298
Kleina	285	348	Kleinpraga	224	298
Kleinbautzen	224	298	Kleinprausitz	285	348
Kleinbernsdorf	251	321	Kleinpresen	224	298
Kleinboblitz	224	298	Kleinradmeritz	234	307
Kleinbobritzsch	263	331	Kleinraschütz	280	343
Kleinbörnchen	263	331	Kleinrennersdorf	290	353
Kleinborthen	290	353	Kleinröhrsdorf	229	303
Kleinbröhsern	224	298		271	339
Kleinburgk	267	335	Kleinrückerswalde	241	315
Kleinburkau	224	298	Kleinrümpf	251	321
	229	303	Kleinschirma	275	341
Kleincarsdorf	264	331	Kleinschönau	237	311
Kleinchursdorf	251	321	Kleinschönberg	285	348
Kleincosmannsdorf	267	335	Kleinschweidnitz	234	307
Kleincotta	290	353	Kleinseidau	224	298
Kleindehsa	234	307	Kleinseitschen	224	298
Kleindittmannsdorf	275	341	Kleinsiderwitz	290	353
Kleindobritz	285	348	Kleinsora	224	298
Kleindöbschütz	224	298	Kleinstruppen	290	353
Kleindorfhain	267	335	Kleinteichnitz	224	298
Kleindrebig	280	343	Kleintetta	234	307
Kleindrebnitz	224	298	Kleinthiermig	280	343
Kleindubrau	224	298	Kleintrebnitz	280	343
Kleinelbersdorf	290	353	Kleinvoigtsberg	275	341
Kleinemühle	255	323	Kleinwaltersdorf	275	341
Kleinerkmannsdorf	271	339	Kleinwelka	224	298
Kleinförstchen	224	298	Kleinwolmsdorf	271	339
Kleingaussig	224	298	Kleinzschachwitz	290	353
Kleingeislitz	280	343	Kleinzschepa	280	343
Kleingieshübel	290	353	Kleppisch	290	354
Kleingraupe	271	339	Klessig	285	348
Kleinhähnchen	224	298	Klinesaubernitz	224	298
Klein Hamburg	267	335	Klingenberg	267	335
Kleinharthau	290	353	Klipphausen	234	307
Kleinhartmannsdorf	247	319		285	348

TOWN	LUTHERAN	CATHOLIC	TOWN	LUTHERAN	CATHOLIC
Klipphäuser	234	307	Krauschütz	280	343
Klix	224	298	Krausitz	285	348
Klostergut	285	348	Krausnitz	280	343
Klosterhäuser	285	348	Krauswitz	285	348
Klosterstrasse	285	348	Krebs	290	354
Klotzsche	290	354	Kreckwitz	224	298
Kmehlen	280	343	Kreiern	285	348
Knaumühle	245	317	Kreinitz	280	343
Kobeln	285	348	Kreischa	264	331
Kobenthal	280	343	Kreischerhof	237	311
Kobitzsch	285	348	Kreissa	285	348
Köblitz	234	307	Krepta	285	348
Kobschien	229	303	Kretzscham		
Kohlau	255	323	Rothensehma	241	315
Kohlmühle	255	323	Kretzschmar		
Kohlosdorf	285	348	Rothensehma	241	315
Kohlung	275	341	Krienitz	224	298
Kohlwesa	234	307	Kriepitz	230	303
Koitsch	229	303	Krieschendorf	271	339
Kolkwitz	280	343	Krieschwitz	290	354
Königsbrück	229	303	Krietzschwitz	290	354
Königshain	237	311	Krinitz	224	298
Königsmühle	224	298	Krippen	290	354
Königstein (Festung)	290	354	Kritzschendorf	271	339
Königstein (Stadt)	290	354	Krobtitz	224	298
Königswalde	241	315	Krögis	285	348
Königswartha	224	298	Kronförstchen	224	298
Koppelsdorf	290	354	Krottendorf	241	315
Kopschin	229	303	Krumhermersdorf	247	319
Körbigsdorf	234	307	Krumhermsdorf	290	354
Korbitz	285	348	Krummenhennersdorf	275	341
Kosakenscheuke	245	317	Krummförstchen	224	298
Koselitz	280	343	Krzewiha	237	311
Kostrzyna	238	312	Kubschütz	224	298
Köthel	251	321	Kuckau	230	303
Kotitz	234	307	Kugelmühlen	224	298
Kötitz	285	348	Kühberg	241	315
Kottewitz	285	348	Kühnast	285	348
Köttewitz	285	348	Kühnhaide	255	323
	290	354		259	327
Kottewitz an der Elbe	280	343	Kuhschnappel	251	321
Kottewitz bei Strauda	280	343	Kumschütz	224	298
Kottmarhäuser	234	307	Kunadmühle	267	335
Kottmarsdorf	234	307	Kunnersdorf	247	319
Kottwitz	285	348	Kupferhammer		
Köttwitz	290	354	in Hüttengrunde	255	323
Kötzschau	234	307	Kuppritz	234	307
Kötzsche	234	307	Kynitzsch	224	298
Kötzschenbroda	271	339			
Krakau	230	303	**L**		
Krappe	234	307			
Krappmühle	230	303	Lampersdorf	275	341
Kratzhammer	264	331	Lampertswalda	280	343
Kraumühle	245	317	Langburkersdorf	290	354

TOWN	LUTHERAN	CATHOLIC	TOWN	LUTHERAN	CATHOLIC
Langebrück	271	339	Leuben	285	348
Langenberg	251	321	Leubnitz	267	335
Langenburkersdorf	290	354	Leubsdorf	247	319
Langenchursdorf	251	321	Leuckersdorf	245	317
Langenhennersdorf	275	341	Leukersdorf	245	317
	290	354	Leupoldishain	290	354
Langenrinne	275	341	Leuterau	237	311
Langenwolmsdorf	290	354	Leuterwitz	267	335
Langenwolmsdorfer			Leutewitz bei Briessnitz	267	335
Schäferei	290	354	Leutewitz bei Meissen	285	348
Langhennersdorf	234	307	Leutewitz bei Riesa	280	343
	290	354	Leutowitz	224	298
Latzke	230	303	Leutswitz	224	298
Lauba	234	307	Lichtenberg	238	311
Laubach	280	343		271	339
Laubegast	285	348		275	341
Lauben bei Weinböhla	285	348	Lichtenhain	290	354
Laucha	234	307	Lichtensee	280	343
Lauenstein	264	331	Lichtenstein	251	321
Lausa	271	339	Lichtenwalde	247	319
Lauske bei Hochkirch	234	307	Lichtewalde	247	319
Lauske bei Hollscha	224	298	Liebau	267	335
Lausnitz	230	303	Liebenau	230	303
Laussnitz	230	303		264	331
Laute	255	323	Liebesdörfel	234	307
Lautendorf	280	343	Liebethal	290	354
Lauterbach	255	323	Liebon	230	303
	280	343	Liebstadt	290	354
	290	354	Liega	280	343
Lautitz	234	307	Liegau	271	339
Lautzschen	285	348	Lieschnitz	285	348
Lawalde	234	307	Lietzke	230	303
Leckwitz	280	343	Limbach	245	317
Lehdenhäuser	237	311		285	348
Lehdenvorwerk	285	348	Linda	275	341
Lehmisch	224	298	Lindenau	271	339
Lehn bei Crostwich	224	298	Lindenberg	234	307
Lehn bei Hochkirch	234	307	Lindicht	285	348
Lehn bei Postwitz	224	298		290	354
Lehndorf	230	303	Lindigt	285	348
Leibnitzdörschen	255	323		290	354
Leibnitzdörschen			Linz	280	343
Mühle	255	323	Lippersdorf	255	323
Leichnam	224	298	Lippitsch	224	298
Leipen	285	348	Lipprandis	251	321
Leippen	285	348	Lissahora	224	298
Leitwitz	224	298	Litten	224	298
Lengefeld	255	323	Litzschnitz	285	348
Lenz	280	343	Löbau	234	307
Leppersdorf	271	339	Löbdau	267	335
Lercha	285	348	Löbenhain	245	317
Leschen	285	348	Löbsal	285	348
Lesten	285	348	Löbschütz		
Letzschmühle	241	315	bei Lommatzsch	285	348

TOWN	LUTHERAN	CATHOLIC	TOWN	LUTHERAN	CATHOLIC
Löbschütz bei Meissen	285	348	Malschendorf	271	339
Lobsdorf	251	321	Malschwitz	225	298
Löbtau	267	335	Malsitz	225	298
Lockwitz	267	335	Malter	264	331
Loga	224	298	Maltermühle	264	331
Lohmen	290	354	Maltitz	234	307
Lohsdorf	290	354	Maltzschendorf	271	339
Lömischau	224	298	Marbach	247	319
Lommatzsch	285	348	Marienberg	255	323
Lomnitz	271	339	Marienborn	230	303
Lomsske	224	298	Marienstern	230	303
Lorenzkirch	280	343	Marienthal	230	303
Lorenzkirchen	280	343	Markeritz	285	348
Löschau	224	298	Markersbach	290	354
Loschwitz	271	339	Markersdorf	238	311
Lossen	285	348		245	317
Lossnitz	275	341	Markocice	238	311
Lössnitz	271	339	Markritz	285	348
	275	341	Marksiedlitz	280	343
Lösten	285	348	Marschau	285	348
Löthain	285	348	Marschitz	285	348
Lotzdorf	271	339	Marschütz	285	348
Lotzen	285	348	Marsdorf	280	343
Lötzschen	280	343	Marterbüschel	255	323
Lotzschmühle	241	315	Mauna	285	348
Luaau	285	348	Mauschwitz	234	307
Lubachau	224	298	Maxdorf	238	311
Lubas	224	298	Maxen	290	354
Lübau	267	335	Medessen	280	343
Luchau	264	331	Medewitz	225	298
Lückendorf	238	311	Medingen	280	343
Lückenhübel			Meerana	251	321
bei Oberspaar	285	348	Mehltheueer	285	348
Lückersdorf	230	303	Mehltheuer	225	298
Ludwigsdorf	251	321		285	348
Lugaerhofschenke	225	298	Mehren	285	348
Lugaerschenke	285	348	Meila	285	348
Lugau	259	327	Meinersdorf	259	327
Lungwitz	264	331	Meinsdorf	251	321
Luppa	225	298	Meissen	285	348
Luppisch Dubrau	225	298	Meisslitz	290	354
Luptin	238	311	Memmendorf	247	319
Lutogniewice	238	312	Mengelsdorfer Mühle	234	307
Lüttewitz bei Leschen	285	348	Merbitz	267	335
Lüttichau	280	343	Mergendorf	280	343
Luttowitz	225	298	Mergenthal	285	348
Lützschen	280	343	Merka	225	298
Lützschnitz	285	348	Merschwitz	280	343
Luxenburg	230	303	Mershwitz	280	343
			Mertitz	285	348
M			Merzdorf	247	319
			Meschwitz	225	298
Mädewitz	225	298		285	348
Mahlitzsch	285	348	Messa	285	348

TOWN	LUTHERAN	CATHOLIC	TOWN	LUTHERAN	CATHOLIC
Mettelwitz	285	348	Mühlbach	247	319
Metzdorf	247	319		280	343
Metzschwitz	285	348		290	354
Meuscha	290	354	Mühlberg	285	348
Meuslitz	290	354	Mühlhäuser	225	298
Meusslitz	290	354	Mühlsdorf	290	354
Micheln	251	321	Mülbitz	280	343
Mickten	271	339	Mulda	275	341
Mikten	271	339	Mülsen St. Jacob	251	321
Milbitz	280	343	Mülsen St. Michaelis	251	321
Mildenau	241	315	Mülsen St. Niclas	251	321
Milkel	225	298	Münchenfrei	275	341
Milkwitz	225	298	Munzig	285	348
Milstrich	230	303	Muschelwitz	225	298
Miltitz	230	303	Mutzschwitz	285	348
	285	348			
Mischwitz	285	348	**N**		
Mittelbach	245	317			
Mittelburkau	225	298	Nadelwitz	225	298
Mittelcunewalde	234	307	Nassau	264	331
Mitteldorf	259	327	Nasseböhla	280	343
Mittelebersbach	280	343	Nauendorf	285	348
Mittelfreidersdorf	234	307	Nauleis	280	343
Mittelherwigsdorf	234	307	Naundorf	241	315
	238	311		290	354
Mittelkreischa	264	331	Naundorf		
Mittelleutersdorf	238	311	bei Bischofswerda	225	298
Mittelmühle	285	348	Naundorf bei Dresden	271	339
Mittelndorf	290	354	Naundorf bei Hain	280	343
Mittelroderwitz	238	311	Naundorf bei Ortrandt	280	343
Mittelrosenhain	234	307	Naundorf bei Pirna	290	354
Mittelsaida	255	323	Naundorf		
Mittelschmiedeberg	241	315	bei Schmiedeberg	264	331
Mittelsohland			Naundorf bei Tharandt	276	341
am Rotstein	234	307	Naundorf bei Zehren	285	348
Mittelsohland			Naundörfchen	280	343
an der Spree	225	298		285	348
Mittelweigsdorf	238	311	Naunhof	280	343
Mittelwolmsdorf	290	354	Nauslitz	230	303
Mobschatz	267	335		267	335
Mockethal	290	354	Nausslitz	230	303
Mockritz	267	335		267	335
Mögen	285	348	Naustadt	285	348
Mohlis	285	348	Nauwalde	280	343
Mohorn	267	335	Nebelschütz	230	303
Möhrsdorf	230	303	Nechern	225	298
Mönchenfrei	275	341	Necheu	234	307
Mönchswalde	225	298	Neckanitz	285	348
Moritz	280	343	Nedaschütz	225	298
Moritzburg	271	339	Neidberg	290	354
Moritzdorf	271	339	Neiderlommatzsch	285	348
Müdisdorf	285	348	Neidhardt	285	348
Mügeln	290	354	Neitschmühle	230	303
Müglitz	264	331	Nelckanitz	285	348

TOWN	LUTHERAN	CATHOLIC	TOWN	LUTHERAN	CATHOLIC
Nelkanitz	285	348	Neueibau	234	307
Nennigmühle	255	323	Neuer Anbau	290	354
Nentmannsdorf	290	354	Neue Schenke	234	307
Neraditz	230	303	Neueulowitz	225	298
Neschwitz	225	298	Neufriedersdorf	234	307
Neuarnsdorf	225	298	Neugeising	264	331
Neubahra	290	354	Neugeorgenfeld	264	331
Neubau	247	319	Neugersdorf		
	264	331	bei Reibersdorf	238	311
	276	341	Neugersdorf		
Neuberthelsdorf	234	307	bei Rumburk	238	311
Neubloaschütz	225	298	Neugraupe	271	339
Neuboblitz	225	298	Neugraupzig	285	348
Neubohlitz	225	298	Neuguhra	225	298
Neuchoren	285	348	Neuhaselbach	255	323
Neucoschütz	267	335	Neuhausen	225	298
Neucunnersdorf	234	307		276	341
Neucunnewitz	234	307	Neuhausmühle	255	323
Neudeck	241	315	Neuhirschstein	285	348
	255	323	Neuhof	225	298
Neudiehmen	225	298		234	307
Neudorf	225	298	Neuhöfchen	285	348
	234	307	Neuhörnitz	238	311
	241	315	Neujohnsdorf	238	311
	267	335	Neukaitz	267	335
	280	343	Neukarcha	285	348
Neudorf an der Spree	225	298	Neukatschwitz	225	298
Neudorf			Neukirch	230	303
bei Königswartha	225	298		285	349
Neudorf bei Lauba	234	307	Neukirch		
Neudorf bei Neschwitz	225	298	bei Königsbrück	230	303
Neudorf			Neukirchen		
bei Schönbach	234	307	bei Chemnitz	245	317
Neudörfchen			Neukirchen		
bei Meissen	285	348	bei Meissen	285	349
Neudörfchen			Neuklingenberg	267	335
bei Sachsenburg	247	319	Neukotitz	234	307
Neudörfel	238	311	Neulanske	225	298
	285	348	Neulauba	234	307
Neudörfel bei Baruth	225	298	Neuleis	280	343
Neudörfel			Neuleutersdorf	238	311
bei Cunewalde	234	307	Neulindenberg	234	307
Neudörfel bei Glashütte	264	331	Neumergenthal	285	349
Neudörfel bei Guttau	225	298	Neuminkwitz	238	311
Neudörfel			Neumühle	225	298
bei Räckelwitz	230	303		255	323
Neudörfel bei Stolpen	290	354	Neundorf	234	307
Neudrauschkowitz	225	298		241	315
Neudresden	267	335		290	354
Neue Haus	241	315	Neunimptsch	267	335
Neue Häuser	225	298	Neuntmannsdorf	290	354
	234	307	Neunzehnhain	247	319
Neue Häuser			Neuoppach	234	307
am Ochsenteich	225	298	Neuoppitz	225	298

TOWN	LUTHERAN	CATHOLIC	TOWN	LUTHERAN	CATHOLIC
Neuostra	267	335	Niederburkersdorf	290	354
Neupurschwitz	225	299	Niedercolmnitz	276	341
Neupuschwitz	225	299	Niedercrostau	225	299
Neuputzkau	225	299	Niedercunewalde	234	308
Neusalza	234	307	Niedercunnersdorf	234	308
Neuscheibe	238	311	Niederdorf	259	327
Neuscheidenbach	225	299	Niederdorfchemnitz	276	341
Neuschirgiswalde	225	299	Niederdornhennersdorf	238	311
Neuschmerlitz	230	303	Niederdrehbach	255	323
Neuschmölln	225	299	Niederebersbach	280	343
Neuschönau	238	311	Niedereula	285	349
Neuschönberg	234	307	Niedereulowitz	225	299
Neuseusslitz	280	343	Niederfähre	285	349
Neusorge	225	299	Niederfedlitz	285	349
	245	317	Niederfehra	285	349
	255	323	Niederforchheim	255	323
	259	327	Niederfraundorf	290	354
	280	343	Niederfriedersdorf	234	308
Neuspreedorf	234	307	Niedergarnsdorf	247	319
Neuspremberg	234	307	Niedergersdorf	230	303
Neustadt	271	339		271	339
	285	349	Niedergohlis	267	335
Neustädtel	230	303	Niedergräfenhain	230	303
Neustadt in Sachsen	290	354	Niedergrumbach	285	349
Neustruppen	290	354	Niedergruna	285	349
Neutanneberg	285	349	Niedergurig	225	299
Neutaubenheim	234	307	Niederhartmannsbach	290	354
Neuwalde	238	311	Niederhaselbach	255	323
Neuwaltersdorf	238	311	Niederhäselich	267	335
Neuwarnsdorf	276	341	Niederhelmsdorf	290	354
Neuweissig	267	335	Niederhermersdorf	267	335
Neuwernsdorf	276	341	Nieder Herwigsdorf	234	307
Neuwiese	259	327	Niederhesslitch	267	335
Neuwunschwitz	285	349	Niederjahna	285	349
Neuzaschendorf	285	349	Niederjahnsbach	264	331
Neuzinnwald	264	331	Niederjohnsbach	264	331
Nickeritz	285	349	Niederkaina	225	299
Nickern	267	335	Niederkemnitz	234	308
Nickolsmühle	285	349	Niederkeyna	225	299
Nickritz	285	349	Niederkiesdorf	234	308
Nicolaimühle	285	349	Niederkittlitz	234	308
Nicolsdorf	290	354	Niederkotitz	234	308
Nieda	238	311	Niederkreischa	264	331
Niederarnsdorf	251	321	Niederlangenau	276	341
Niederau	285	349	Niederlauba	234	308
Nieder Auerswalde	247	319	Niederlauterstein	255	323
Niederbeiersdorf	234	307	Niederlawalde	234	308
Niederbelbitz	234	307	Niederleuba	238	311
Niederberthelsdorf	234	307	Niederleutersdorf	238	311
Niederbischdorf	234	307	Niederlichtenau	230	303
Niederbobritzsch	276	341		247	319
Niederboiritz	271	339	Niederlockwitz	267	335
Niederburka	225	299	Niederlössnitz	271	339
Niederburkau	225	299	Niederlungwitz	251	321

378

TOWN	LUTHERAN	CATHOLIC	TOWN	LUTHERAN	CATHOLIC
Niedermalschwitz	225	299	Niedertaubenheim	234	308
Niedermalter	264	331		285	349
Niedermeusegast	290	354	Niedertoppschedel	285	349
Niedermühlbach	247	319	Niederuhna	225	299
Niedermülsen	251	321	Niederulbersdorf	290	354
Niedermuschitz	285	349	Niedervogelsang	290	354
Niedermuschütz	285	349	Niedervoigtsdorf	276	341
Niedernatzschkau	255	323	Niederwanscha	238	311
Niedernatzschung	255	323	Niederwartha	285	349
Niederneukirch			Niederweigsdorf	238	311
am Hochwalde	225	299	Niederwiesa	247	319
Niederneuschönberg	276	341	Niederwinkel	251	321
Niederolbersdorf	238	311	Niederwolmsdorf	290	354
Niederoppach	234	308	Niederwürschnitz	259	327
Niederottendorf	290	354	Niederzschanitz	280	343
Niederottenhain	234	308	Niederzwönitz	259	327
Niederpesterwitz	267	335	Niedów	238	311
Niederpöbel	264	331	Niegerode	280	343
Niederpoiritz	271	339	Nieschütz	286	349
Niederpolenz	285	349	Niesendorf	225	299
Niederposta	290	354	Nieska	280	343
Niederpoyritz	271	339	Niethen	234	308
Niederpretzschendorf	264	331	Niethener Mühle	234	308
Niederputzkau	225	299	Nimschütz	225	299
Niederrabenstein	245	317	Nimtitz	286	349
Niederrathen	290	354	Ninive	234	308
Niederreichstädt	264	331	Nischütz	286	349
Niederreinhardtsgrimma	264	331	Nödaschütz	225	299
Niederreinsberg	285	349	Noselitz	286	349
Niederrennersdorf	234	308	Nossen	286	349
Niederrochwitz	271	339	Nössge	286	349
Niederrödern	280	343	Nössige	286	349
Niederroderwitz	238	311	Nosslitz	286	349
Niederruppersdorf	234	308	Nostitz	234	308
Niedersaida	255	323	Nöthnitz	267	335
Niederschindelbach	255	323	Nucknitz	230	303
Niederschlag	241	315	Nüncheritz	280	343
Niederschmiedeberg	241	315	Nünchritz	280	343
Niederschmölln	225	299	Nundörfel	286	349
Niederschöna	276	341	Nutzung	252	321
Niederschönbach	234	308			
Niederseida	255	323	**O**		
Niederseidewitz	290	354			
Niederseifenbach	276	341	Oberau	286	349
Niederseyffenbach	276	341	Oberauerswalde	247	319
Niedersohlan			Oberbahra	290	354
an der Spree	225	299	Oberbeiersdorf	234	308
Niedersohland			Oberbelbitz	234	308
am Rotstein	234	308	Oberberthelsdorf	234	308
Niederspaar	285	349	Oberbischdorf	234	308
Niederspremberg	234	308	Oberbobritzsch	276	341
Niederstaucha	285	349	Oberboiritz	271	339
Niedersteina	230	303	Oberburkau	225	299
Niederstrahwalde	234	308	Oberburkersdorf	291	354

TOWN	LUTHERAN	CATHOLIC	TOWN	LUTHERAN	CATHOLIC
Obercolmnitz	276	341	Oberleuba	238	311
Obercrostau	225	299	Oberleutersdorf	238	311
Obercunewalde	234	308	Oberlichtenau	230	303
Obercunnersdorf	234	308		247	319
	264	331	Oberlockwitz	267	335
Oberdöhlen	267	335	Oberlommatzsch	286	349
Oberdorf	241	315	Oberlössnitz	271	339
	252	321	Oberlöwenhain	264	331
	259	327	Oberlungwitz	252	321
Oberdorfchemnitz	276	341	Obermalschwitz	225	299
Oberdornhennersdorf	238	311	Obermalter	264	331
Oberdrehbach	255	323	Obermeisa	286	349
Oberebersbach	280	343	Obermeusegast	291	354
Obereula	286	349	Obermühlbach	247	319
Obereulowitz	225	299	Obermuschitz	286	349
Oberforchheim	255	323	Obernatzschkau	256	323
Oberförstchen	225	299	Obernatzschung	256	323
Oberfraundorf	264	331	Obernaundorf	264	331
Oberfrohna	245	317	Oberndorf	241	315
Obergarnsdorf	247	319		252	321
Obergersdorf	230	303	Oberneukirch		
	271	339	am Hochwalde	225	299
Obergohlis	267	335	Oberneuschönberg	276	341
Obergorbitz	267	335	Oberoderwitz	234	308
Obergräfenhain	230	303	Oberolbersdorf	238	311
Obergrumbach	286	349	Oberoppach	234	308
Obergruna	286	349	Oberottendorf	291	354
Obergurig	225	299	Oberottenhain	234	308
Obergurk	225	299	Oberpesterwitz	267	335
Obergurkau	225	299	Oberpoiritz	271	339
Oberhartmannsbach	291	354	Oberpolenz	286	349
Oberhaselbach	256	323	Oberposta	291	354
Oberhässlich	264	331	Oberpoyritz	271	339
Oberhelmsdorf	291	354	Oberpretzschendorf	264	331
Oberhermersdorf	245	317	Oberputzkau	225	299
Oberhermsdorf	286	349	Oberrabenstein	245	317
Oberherwigsdorf	234	308	Oberrathen	291	354
Oberherwigsdorf			Oberreichenbach	276	341
bei Zittau	238	311	Oberreichstädt	264	331
Oberhesslich	264	331	Oberreinhardtsgrimma	264	331
Oberhütte	291	354	Oberreinsberg	286	349
Oberjahna	286	349	Oberrennersdorf	234	308
Oberjohnsbach	264	331	Oberrochwitz	271	339
Oberkaina	225	299	Oberrödern	280	344
Oberkarsdorf	264	331	Oberruppersdorf	234	308
Oberkeina	225	299	Obersaida	256	323
Oberkemnitz	234	308	Oberschaar	241	315
Oberkiesdorf	234	308		276	341
Oberkittlitz	234	308	Oberscheibe	241	315
Oberkotitz	234	308	Oberscheube	241	315
Oberkreischa	264	331	Oberschindelbach	256	323
Oberlangenau	276	341	Oberschindmaas	252	321
Oberlauba	234	308	Oberschlottewitz	286	349
Oberlawalde	234	308	Oberschmiedeberg	256	323

TOWN	LUTHERAN	CATHOLIC	TOWN	LUTHERAN	CATHOLIC
Oberschmölln	225	299	Oertelsdorf	247	319
Oberschöna	276	341	Oertelshain	252	321
Oberschönbach	234	308	Ohorn	230	303
Oberseida	256	323	Okrilla	272	339
Oberseidewitz	291	354		286	349
Oberseifenbach	276	341	Olbernhau	256	323
Oberseifersdorf	238	311	Olbersdorf	238	311
Oberseiffenbach	276	341		245	317
Obersohland			Omsewitz	267	335
am Rotstein	234	308	Opolno Zdrój	238	312
Obersohland			Oppach	234	308
an der Spree	225	299	Oppeln	234	308
Oberspaar	286	349	Oppelsdorf	238	312
Oberspremberg	234	308	Oppitz	225	299
Oberstaucha	286	349	Ortelsdorf	247	319
Obersteina	230	303	Ossel	230	303
Obersteinbach	286	349	Ossling	230	303
Oberstötzwitz	286	349	Ostra	267	335
Oberstrahwalde	234	308	Ostrau	291	354
Obertaubenheim	234	308	Ostritz	238	312
	286	349	Ostro	230	303
Obertoppschedel	286	349	Ottenbach	286	349
Oberuhna	225	299	Ottendorf	272	339
Oberulbersdorf	291	354		291	354
Oberullersdorf	238	311	Otterschütz	230	303
Obervogelgesang	291	354	Ottowalde	291	354
Obervoigtsdorf	276	341	Oybin	238	312
Oberwanscha	238	311			
Oberwartha	267	335	**P**		
Oberweigsdorf	238	311			
Oberweissig	267	335	Pabstdorf	291	354
Oberwiehra	252	321	Pahrenz	286	349
Oberwiera	252	321	Paltzschen	286	349
Oberwiesa	247	319	Panisdorf	264	331
Oberwiesenthal	241	315	Panishain	264	331
Oberwinkel	252	321	Pannewitz am Taucher	225	299
Oberwolmsdorf	291	354	Pannewitz bei Weidlitz	225	299
Oberwürschnitz	259	327	Papperitz	272	339
Oberwyhra	252	321	Papstdorf	291	354
Oberzehren	286	349	Parostensa	230	304
Oberzschanitz	280	344	Passditz	230	304
Obverpöbel	264	331	Pasternik	238	312
Ockerwitz	267	335	Pathen	225	299
Ockrilla	286	349	Pattersleben	280	344
Oederan	247	319	Paulsmühle	280	344
Oehlisch	234	308	Pauschütz	286	349
Oehna	225	299	Pauschwitz	230	304
Oelisch	234	308	Pausitz	286	349
Oelsa	234	308	Pegenau	286	349
Oelsen	291	354	Pelzmühle	245	317
Oelsengrund	291	354	Pelzmusche	234	308
Oelsitz	286	349	Pennrich	267	335
Oelsnitz	259	327	Perba	286	349
	280	344	Peritz	280	344
			Perne	286	349

TOWN	LUTHERAN	CATHOLIC	TOWN	LUTHERAN	CATHOLIC
Peschelmühle	286	349	Porschberg	272	339
Peschen	234	308	Porschdorf	291	354
Pesterwitz	267	335	Porschendorf	247	319
Petersbach	225	299		291	354
Petersberg	286	349	Porschnitz	286	349
Petershain	230	304	Porschütz	280	344
Pethau	238	312	Porsdorf	286	349
Petzschwitz	286	349	Posada	238	312
Pfaffendorf	291	354	Posewitz	291	354
Pfaffroda	252	321	Possendorf	264	331
	276	341	Pössighaus	286	349
Picka	234	308	Postelwitz	291	354
Pickau	225	299	Posthorn	291	354
Pielitz	225	299	Postschenke	225	299
Pieschen	272	339	Postswitz	225	299
Piesskowitz	230	304	Potitz	286	349
Pietzschwitz	225	299	Pottschappel	268	335
Pillnitz	272	339	Pottschapplitz	225	299
Pillsdorf	276	341	Pötzscha	291	354
Pilsdorf	276	341	Prabschütz	268	335
Pinckwitz	286	349	Praschwitz	225	299
Pinkowitz	286	349	Praterschütz	286	349
Pinnewitz	286	349	Pratzschwitz	291	354
Pirmenitz	286	349	Prausitz	286	349
Pirna	291	354	Prautitz	230	304
Piskowitz	230	304	Preishaus	241	315
Piskowitz bei Hain	280	344	Preititz	225	299
Piskowitz bei Schieritz	286	349	Preske	225	299
Piskowitz			Pretzsch	268	335
bei Taubenheim	286	349	Preuschwitz	225	299
Pitzschütz	286	349	Priesa	286	349
Planitz	286	349	Priesen	286	349
Plänitz	286	349	Priessgen	264	331
Plankenstein	286	349	Priestewitz	280	344
Plaue	247	319	Prietitz	230	304
Plauen	268	335	Prischwitz	225	299
Pleisa	245	317	Pritzschwitz	225	299
Pleissa	245	317	Pröda bei Meissen	286	349
Pliesskowitz	225	299	Pröda bei Schleinitz	286	349
Ploschwitz	291	354	Prohlis	268	335
Plotzenhäuser	234	308	Promnitz	280	344
	286	349	Proschwitz	286	349
Pobershau	256	323	Prositz bei Schieritz	286	349
Pockau	256	323	Prositz bei Staucha	286	349
Podemus	268	335	Prossen	291	354
Poderitz	268	335	Prössgen	264	331
Pohla	225	299	Pröstewitz	280	344
Pöhsig	286	349	Pulsen	280	344
Poititz	286	349	Pultznitz	230	304
Polenz	291	354	Purschenstein	276	341
Poltzschen	286	349	Purschwitz	225	299
Pommritz	225	299	Puscheritz	225	299
Ponickau	280	344	Puschwitz	225	299
Poppitz	280	344	Putzkau	225	299

TOWN	LUTHERAN	CATHOLIC	TOWN	LUTHERAN	CATHOLIC
Q			Reichenau	230	304
				238	312
Quatitz	225	299		264	331
Queris	280	344	Reichenbach	230	304
Querse	280	344	Reichenbach		
Questenberg	286	349	bei Hohenstein	252	321
Quohren bei Bühlau	272	339	Reichenbach bei		
Quohren bei Kreischa	264	331	Langenhennersdorf	276	341
Quoos	225	299	Reichenbach		
Quosdorf	230	304	bei Scharfenberg	286	349
			Reichenberg	272	339
R			Reichenbrand	245	317
			Reichenhain	245	317
Rabenau	268	335	Reichenheim	245	317
Rabitz	225	299	Reichstädt	264	331
Rackel	225	299	Reichstein	264	331
Räckelwitz	230	304	Reick	268	335
Räcknitz	268	335	Reifland	256	323
Radeberg	272	339	Reinberg	264	331
Radebeul	272	339	Reinersdorf	280	344
Radeburg	272	339	Reinhardtsdorf	291	354
Raden	280	344	Reinhardtsgrimma	264	331
Radewitz	286	349	Reinholdshain	252	321
Radgendorf	238	312	Reinitz	230	304
Radibor	225	299	Reisewitz	268	335
Radmeritz	234	308	Reissigmühle	256	323
Radwitz	280	344	Reitzendorf	272	339
Rähnitz	272	339	Reitzenhain	256	323
Ralbitz	230	304	Remissen	252	321
Rammenau	225	299	Remse	252	321
Randeck	286	349	Rennersdorf		
Räsa	286	349	bei Stolpen	291	354
Raschau	225	299	Rennersdorf		
Rasslitz	286	349	bei Wilsdruf	268	335
Rathen	291	354	Reppina	286	349
Rathewalde	291	354	Reppis	280	344
Rathmannsdorf	291	354	Reppnitz	286	349
Rattwitz	225	299	Reuckersdorf	276	341
Raube	286	349	Reuterhaus	241	315
Rauenstein	256	323	Reutnitz	238	312
Rauenthal	286	349	Rhäsa	286	349
Raum	241	315	Rhensdorf	230	304
	291	354	Richtermühle	245	317
Raummühle	241	315		247	319
Rauschenbach	276	341		259	327
Rauschwitz	230	304	Riemsdorf	286	349
Rausslitz	286	349	Riesa	280	344
Rechenberg	264	331	Rieschen	225	299
Rectormühle	252	321	Ringenhain	225	299
Rehefeld	264	331	Rippien	264	331
Rehfeld	264	331	Rittersberg	256	323
Rehnsdorf	230	304	Robschütz	286	349
Reibersdorf	238	312	Rockau	272	339
Reichbach	252	321	Roda bei Hain	280	344

TOWN	LUTHERAN	CATHOLIC	TOWN	LUTHERAN	CATHOLIC
Röderau	280	344	Rüssdorf	252	321
Röderbrunn	225	299	Rüsseina	286	349
Rödern	280	344	Rybarzowice	238	312
Rodewitz bei Crostau	225	299			
Rodewitz bei Hochkirch	234	308	**S**		
Rödlitz	252	321			
Rohna	225	299	Saalendorf	238	312
Rohnau	238	312	Saalhausen	268	335
Rohrbach	230	304	Sachsdorf	286	349
Röhrsdorf	230	304	Sachsenburg	247	319
	245	317	Sachsenhof	276	341
	286	349	Sächsische Reuter	225	299
Roitzsch bei Dresden	286	349	Sachsmüuhle	241	315
Roitzsch bei Oschatz	286	349	Sacka	280	344
Roitzschberg	286	349	Sadisdorf	264	331
Roitzschen	286	349	Sageritz	280	344
Roitzschwiese	286	349	Sahlendorf	238	312
Romerei	238	312	Saida	264	331
Ronaw	238	312		276	341
Röschen	225	299	Saigerhütte Grünthal	256	323
Rosenhain	234	308	Salga	225	299
Rosenthal	230	304	Salhausen	268	335
	238	312	Salzenforst	225	299
	291	354	Salzforstchen	225	299
Rosentitz	268	335	Sand	276	341
Rossendorf	291	354	Sankt Egidien	252	321
Rossthal	268	335	Sankt Michaelis	276	341
Rostig	280	344	Särchen	225	299
Rothenbach	252	321	Saritzsch	225	299
Röthenbach	264	331	Särka	234	308
Rothenfurth	276	341	Satzung	256	323
Rothenhammer			Saultitz	286	349
bei Wiesenthal	241	315	Saupsdorf	291	354
Rothenthal	256	323	Säuritz	230	304
Rothnauslig	225	299	Saxdorf	286	349
Rothschönberg	286	349	Sayda	276	341
Rothwernsdorf	291	354	Schafflegen	259	327
Rottewitz	286	349	Schäller	252	321
Rottluf	245	317	Schandau	291	354
Rottwerndorf	291	354	Schänitz bei Riesa	286	349
Rubelschütz	225	299	Schänitz bei Schleinitz	286	349
Rübenau	256	323	Scharfenberg	286	349
Rückenhain	264	331	Scharfenstein	256	323
Rückersdorf	291	354	Scharre	238	312
Rückerswalde	256	323	Schaudorf	225	299
Rudolphsdorf	264	331	Scheckichtmühle	230	304
Rudolphsmühle	252	321	Scheckwitz	226	299
Rugiswalde	291	354	Scheerau	286	349
Ruhethal	225	299	Scheibe	238	312
Rümpf	252	321		245	317
Ruppendorf	264	331	Scheibe bei Frohnau	241	315
Rusdorf	238	312	Scheibe bei Schönbrunn	256	323
Rüsdorf	252	321	Scheibenberg	241	315
Russdorf	238	312	Scheibenmühle	256	323

TOWN	LUTHERAN	CATHOLIC	TOWN	LUTHERAN	CATHOLIC
Scheidebach	256	323		272	339
Scheidenbach	226	299		280	344
Schellenberg	247	319	Schönbörnchen	252	321
Schellerhau	264	332	Schönbörngen	252	321
Schellermühle	264	332	Schönbrunn	226	299
Scherau	286	349	Schönbrunn		
Scherfmühle	259	327	bei Dresden	268	336
Schickenmühle	256	323	Schönbrunn bei		
Schiefermühle	252	321	Grosshennersdorf	235	308
Schieritz	286	349	Schönbrunn		
Schindelbach	256	323	bei Radeberg	272	339
Schirgiswalde	226	299	Schönbrunn		
Schlegel	238	312	zum Dresden	268	336
Schleinitz	286	349	Schönerstadt	248	319
Schletta	286	349	Schönfeld	238	312
Schlettau	241	315		241	315
Schlettemühle	256	323		264	332
Schlettheim	259	327		272	339
Schliefermühle	226	299		276	341
Schloss Chemnitz	245	317		280	344
Schlösschen	247	319	Schönnbrunn		
Schlössel	241	315	bei Wolkenstein	256	324
Schlösselmühle	248	319	Schönnewitz	286	349
Schlossmühle	256	323	Schrebitz bei Nossen	286	349
Schlottwitz	264	332	Schullwitz	272	339
Schlottwitzer	291	354	Schützenhof	241	315
Schlottwitzer Hütten	291	354	Schwaben	252	321
Schlungwitz	226	299	Schwarzmühle	245	317
Schlunzig	252	321		248	319
Schmalzgrube	241	315	Schwarznauslitz	226	299
Schmeckwitz	230	304	Schwarzwasser	226	299
Schmerlitz	230	304	Schwedei	248	319
Schmiedeberg	264	332	Schweinerden	230	304
Schmiedefeld	291	354	Schweinfurth	280	344
Schmiedewalde	286	349	Schweinsdorf	268	336
Schmilka	291	354	Schwepnitz	230	304
Schmochtitz	226	299	Schweppnitz	230	304
Schmohla	226	299	Schwettei	248	319
Schmole	226	299	Schwochau	286	349
Schmölln	226	299	Schwoosdorf	230	304
Schmorkau	230	304	Sdier	226	299
Schmörlitz	230	304	Sebnitz	291	354
Schmorsdorf	291	354	Sebschütz	286	349
Schöna	291	354	Seebschütz	286	349
Schönau	245	317	Seeligstadt	286	349
Schönau				291	354
auf dem Eigen	234	308	Seelingstadt	286	349
Schönau bei Kamenz	230	304	Sehma	241	315
Schönbach	230	304	Seida	264	332
	235	308	Seidau	226	299
	291	354	Seidichen	264	332
Schönberg	235	308	Seidnitz	286	349
	252	321	Seifen	264	332
Schönborn	248	319		276	341

TOWN	LUTHERAN	CATHOLIC	TOWN	LUTHERAN	CATHOLIC
Seiferitz	252	321	Soppen	286	350
Seifersdorf	259	327	Sora	226	299
Seifersdorf				276	341
bei Dippoldiswalde	264	332		286	350
Seifersdorf bei Freiberg	276	341	Sorgau	256	324
Seiffen	276	341	Sorge	245	317
Seifhennersdorf	238	312	Sorgenfrei	264	332
Seilitz	286	350	Sorgenmühle	242	315
Seitendorf	235	308	Soritz	226	299
	238	312	Sörnewitz	286	350
Seitenhain	291	354	Sornitz	286	350
Seitgendorf	238	312	Sornssig	226	299
Seitnitz	286	350	Sosa	286	350
Seligstadt	291	354	Spansberg	280	344
Sella	230	304	Spechtritz	264	332
Selle	230	304	Spechtshausen	268	336
Semichau	226	299	Spittel bei Kamenz	230	304
Semmelsberg	286	350	Spittel bei Weissenberg	235	308
Senfenhammer	255	323	Spittewitz	286	350
Serkowitz	272	339	Spittwitz	226	299
Sernewitz	286	350	Spitzgrund	286	350
Seuritz	226	299	Spitzkunnersdorf	238	312
Seusslitz	280	344	Sporbitz	291	354
Siebeneichen	286	350	Spreedorf	235	308
Siebenhöfen	242	315	Spremberg	235	308
Siebenlehn	286	350	Spytków	238	311
Siebitz bei Göda	226	299		238	312
Siebitz bei Marienstern	226	299	Stacha	226	299
Sieglitz bei Klappendorf	286	350	Stahlberg	242	315
Sieglitz bei Meissen	286	350	Stahna	286	350
Siegmar	245	317	Stangendorf	252	321
Silbergrube	259	327	Starrbach	286	350
Singwitz	226	299	Staucha	286	350
Sinkwitz	226	299	Stauda	280	344
Skala	226	299	Stegvorwerk	248	319
Skassa	280	344	Steinbach		
Skässchen	280	344	bei Annaberg	256	324
Skässgen	280	344	Steinbach		
Skasske	230	304	bei Kesselsdorf	286	350
Skaup	280	344	Steinbach bei Mohorn	286	350
Sobrigau	268	336	Steinbach		
Söbrigen	272	339	bei Moritzburg	280	344
Soeulahora	226	299	Steinbachmühle	245	317
Söhnitz	286	350	Steinberg	256	324
Sohra	226	299	Steinborn	230	304
	276	341	Steindörfel	226	299
Sollschwitz	226	299	Steinigtwolmsdorf	226	299
Sommerau	238	312	Stelzendorf	245	317
Sommerluga	230	304	Stenz	230	304
Somsdorf	268	336	Sternmühle	245	317
Sönitz	286	350	Stetzsch	268	336
Sonnenberg	226	299	Steudten	286	350
	235	308	Steyermühle	286	350
Sonnenstein	291	354	Stiebitz	226	299

TOWN	LUTHERAN	CATHOLIC	TOWN	LUTHERAN	CATHOLIC
Stiesen	280	344	Thalheim	259	327
Stillerode	226	299	Tharandt	268	336
Stollberg	259	327	Theisewitz	264	332
Stolpen	291	354	Thiemendorf	230	304
Stölpgen	280	344		248	319
Stolzenhain	256	324	Thiendorf	281	344
Storcha	226	299	Thiergarten	252	321
Storchnest	245	317		291	354
Strand	291	354	Thronitz	291	354
Strassgräbchen	230	304	Thum	242	315
Strauch	280	344	Thumitz	226	299
Streckewalde	242	315	Thurm	252	321
Strehla	226	299	Thürmsdorf	291	354
Strehlen	268	336	Tiefenau	281	344
Streitfeld	235	308	Tiefendorf	235	308
Streumen	281	344	Tirschheim	252	321
Striegnitz	286	350	Tolkewitz	287	350
Striesen	268	336	Torna	268	336
	281	344	Trachau	272	339
Stroga	281	344	Trachenberge	272	339
Strohschütz	226	299	Trado	230	304
Stroischen	286	350	Tradow	230	304
Struppen	291	354	Trattlau	238	312
Strzegomice	237	311	Trauschwitz	235	308
Stürza	291	354	Treben	287	350
Süppe	226	299	Trebigau	226	299
Suppo	226	299	Trebnitz	235	308
Sürsen	291	354	Trebnitzmühle	291	354
Sützenbach	276	341	Treugeböhla	281	344
			Triebischhäuser	287	350
T			Tröbigau	226	299
			Trogen	287	350
Talpenberg	230	304	Tronitz	287	350
Tannaberg	242	315		291	354
Tanneberg	287	350	Truppen	226	299
Tannenberg	242	315	Trützschler	252	321
Tannenmühle	248	319	Trzciniec	238	312
Taschendorf	226	299	Tscharnitz	226	299
Taubenheim	287	350	Tschaschwitz	226	299
Tauscha	281	344	Tschorna bei Lauske	235	308
Tauschermühle	259	327	Tschornau bei Kamenz	230	304
Tautewalde	226	299	Türchau	238	312
Techritz	226	299	Turoszów	238	312
Teicha	226	299	Tuttendorf	276	341
Teichhäuser	226	299			
Teichmühle	281	344	**U**		
Teichnitz	226	299			
Teichvorwerk	256	324	Uebigau	226	300
Tellerhäuser am Kaff	242	315		272	339
Temmritz	226	299		281	344
Tempel	252	321	Uhlmannsdorf	252	321
	256	324	Uhyst am Taucher	226	300
Temritz	226	299	Uibigau	272	339
Tettau	252	321		281	344

TOWN	LUTHERAN	CATHOLIC	TOWN	LUTHERAN	CATHOLIC
Ulberndorf	264	332	Wantewitz	281	344
Ulbersdorf	291	354	Wartha	226	300
Ullendorf	287	350	Wasserburg	287	350
Ullersdorf	272	339	Wassergrund	235	308
	276	341	Wasserkretscham	235	308
Unckersdorf	287	350	Wauden	287	350
Unsewitz	268	336	Wawitz	226	300
Unterlöwenhain	264	332	Weesenstein	291	354
Untermühle	242	315	Wegefarth	276	341
Unterweissig	268	336	Wehlen	291	354
Unterwiesenthal	241	315	Wehlstädtel	291	354
	242	315	Wehrsdorf	226	300
Unterzehren	287	350	Weicha	226	300
Unwürde	235	308	Weicholdswälder		
Ursprung	259	327	Vorwerke	264	332
Uttewalde	291	354	Weickersdorf	226	300
			Weida	281	344
V			Weide	256	324
			Weidensdorf	252	321
Venusberg	256	324	Weidlitz	226	300
Vogelgesang	226	300	Weigmannsdorf	276	341
	287	350	Weigsdorf im Gebirge	235	308
Voigtlaide	252	321	Weikersdorf	272	339
Voigtsdorf	276	341	Weinböhla	287	350
Voldern	281	344	Weindischfehra	291	355
Volkersdorf	281	344	Weinwiese	252	321
Vorbrücke	287	350	Weisa	226	300
Vordercoffebaude	268	336	Weisenborn	276	341
			Weissbach		
W			bei Königsbrück	230	304
			Weissbach		
Wachau	272	339	bei Pulssnitz	230	304
Wachtnitz	287	350	Weissbach		
Wachwitz	272	339	bei Zschopau	248	319
Waditz	226	300	Weissenberg	235	308
Wagenbach	256	324	Weissenborn	276	341
Wahnitz	287	350	Weissig	268	336
Wahnsdorf	272	339	Weissig am Raschütz	281	344
Waizdorf	291	354	Weissig bei Bautzen	226	300
Wald	238	312	Weissig bei Biehla	272	339
Walda	281	344	Weissig bei Kamenz	230	304
Walddorf	235	308	Weissig bei Königstein	291	355
Walddörfchen	291	354	Weissig bei Skassa	281	344
Waldenburg	252	321	Weissnauslitz	226	300
Waldkirchen	248	319	Weisstropp	287	350
Waldschenke	245	317	Weitzschen	287	350
Wallroda	272	339	Weixdorf	272	339
Waltersdorf	238	312	Welka bei Pulssnitz	230	304
	242	315	Welkau	226	300
	264	332	Wellixande	281	344
	276	341	Welschhufe	264	332
	291	354	Welxande	281	344
Walthersdorf	242	315	Wendischbaselitz	230	304
	264	332	Wendischbora	287	350
Wanscha	238	312			

TOWN	LUTHERAN	CATHOLIC	TOWN	LUTHERAN	CATHOLIC
Wendischcunnersdorf	235	308	Wolka	287	350
Wendischenbohra	287	350	Wölka	291	355
Wendischkarsdorf	264	332	Wolkau	287	350
Wendischpaulsdorf	235	308	Wölkau	226	300
Wendischsohland	226	300		291	355
Wernsdorf bei Glauchau	252	321	Wolkenstein	256	324
Wesenstein	291	355	Wölkisch	287	350
Wesnitz	281	344	Wölknitz	281	344
Wessel	226	300	Worbs	226	300
Wessnitzmühle	226	300	Wuhnitz	287	350
Wetro	226	300	Wuhsen	287	350
Wettersdorf	287	350	Wuischke bei Gröditz	226	300
Wetterwitz	287	350	Wuischke bei Hochkirch	235	308
Wichstanda	281	344	Wuischker Mühle	226	300
Wickersdorf	252	321	Wülknitz	281	344
Wiednitzer	230	304	Wünschendorf	252	321
Wiesa	230	304		256	324
	242	315		291	355
Wiesenbad	242	315	Wunschwitz	287	350
Wiesenmühle	226	300	Wurbis	226	300
	256	324	Wurgwitz	287	350
Wiesenthal	238	312	Wurschen	226	300
Wietrau	226	300	Würschnitz	272	339
Wigancice Żytawskie	238	311		281	344
Wildberg	287	350	Wüstanda	281	344
Wildenburg	256	324	Wüstenbrand	245	317
Wildenhain	281	344	Wüstenschlette	256	324
Wildhaus	256	324	Wüsteschlette	256	324
Wilischthal	248	319	Wüsthetzdorf	276	341
Wilmsdorf	264	332	Wyszków	238	311
Wilsch	256	324			
Wilschdorf	291	355	**Z**		
Wilschwitz	287	350			
Wilsdruf	287	350	Zabeltitz	281	344
Wilsdruff	287	350	Zadel	287	350
Wilthen	226	300	Zaschendorf	272	339
Wind	245	317	Zatonie	238	312
Windorf	287	350	Zatzschke	291	355
Windschenke	238	312	Zaukerode	268	336
Wingendorf	248	319	Zaunhaus	264	332
	291	355	Zehista	291	355
Winkwitz	287	350	Zehmen'sches Gut	287	350
Wittgendorf	238	312	Zehren	287	350
	264	332	Zeichen	291	355
Witzschdorf	248	319	Zeisholz	230	304
Witzschendorf	248	319	Zeissholz	230	304
Wohla bei Löbau	235	308	Zeithain	281	344
Wohla bei Pulssnitz	230	304	Zellmen	268	336
Wölfnitz	268	336	Zerna	226	300
Wolfsberg	256	324	Zescha	226	300
Wolfsberg bei Neusorge	248	319	Zeschnig	291	355
Wolfschmiede	242	315	Zethau	276	341
Wolfsgrün	287	350	Zetta	287	350
Wolfsgrund	276	341	Zettelhaus	242	315

TOWN	LUTHERAN	CATHOLIC	TOWN	LUTHERAN	CATHOLIC
Zetzsch	287	350	Zschärtnitz	268	336
Ziegelgrund	235	308	Zschaschwitz	226	300
Ziegelheim	252	321	Zscheckwitz	264	332
Ziegelschenne	226	300	Zscheila	287	350
	256	324	Zscheilitz	287	350
Ziegeluhlsdorf	252	321	Zscheisewitz	291	355
Ziegenhain	287	350	Zschepa	281	344
Zieglerthal	235	308	Zschertnitz	268	336
Zieschen	281	344	Zschiedge	268	336
Zieschütz	226	300	Zschieren	291	355
Zietsch	230	304	Zschieschen	281	344
Zinnwald	264	332	Zschillchau	226	300
Zischkowitz	226	300	Zschillichau	226	300
Zittau	238	312	Zschochau	287	350
Zittel	238	312	Zschopau	248	319
Zitzschewig	272	339	Zschopenthal	248	319
Zoblitz	235	308	Zschorna	235	308
Zöblitz	256	324	Zschorna bei Radeburg	281	344
Zochau	230	304	Zschornau	230	304
Zockau	226	300	Zschornmühle	281	344
Zollhaus Berghäusel	242	315	Zuckmantel	235	308
Zöllmen	268	336	zum Steiger	268	336
Zöthain	287	350	Zuschendorf	291	355
Zottewitz	281	344	Zwiesel	291	355
Zschäckwitz	264	332	Zwirzschka	291	355
Zschaiten	281	344	Zwönitz	259	327
Zschanitz	281	344			

KINGDOM OF SAXONY
Parts I and II - Master Index

LOCALITY	PART	LOCALITY	PART	LOCALITY	PART
Bennewitz	Part I	Birkwitz	Part II	Börln	Part I
Berba	Part II	Birmenitz	Part II	Borna	Part I, II
Berbersdorf	Part I	Bischdorf	Part II	Bornau	Part II
Berbisdorf	Part II	Bischheim	Part II	Börnchen	Part II
Berenbach	Part II	Bischofswerda	Part II	Börnersdorf	Part II
Berg beim Hetschenhaus	Part I	Bischofswiese	Part I	Börnichen bei Oederan	Part II
Berge	Part II	Bischwiese	Part I	Börnichen bei Zschorau	Part II
Bergen bei Adorf	Part I	Bitthaus	Part I	Bornitz	Part I, II
Bergen bei Trieb	Part I	Bitthäusel	Part I	Bornitz bei Lommatzsch	Part II
Bergfreiheit bei Aue	Part I	Blankenhain	Part I	Borsberg	Part II
Bergfreiheit bei Neustädtel	Part I	Blankenstein	Part II	Borschütz	Part II
Bergfreiheit bei Schneeberg	Part I	Blattersleben	Part II	Borsdorf	Part I
Berggieshübel	Part II	Blauer Stern	Part II	Borstendorf	Part II
Berggut	Part II	Blaufarbenwerk	Part I	Bortewitz	Part I
Berghäusel	Part II	Bloaschütz	Part II	Börtewitz	Part I
Berghäuser	Part II	Blochwitz	Part II	Borthen	Part II
Berghäuser bei Gopplasgrün	Part I	Blösa	Part II	Bösdorf	Part I
Berghäuser bei Stolpen	Part II	Blossenberg	Part I	Bösenbrunn	Part I
Bergisdorf	Part I	Blosswitz	Part I	Bosengröba	Part I
Bergkeller	Part I	Blumberg	Part I, II	Bösengröba	Part I
Berglas	Part I	Blumenau	Part II	Bosenhof	Part I
Bergmühle	Part II	Blumenhof	Part II	Bosewitz	Part II
Bergscheuke	Part I	Blumroda	Part I	Bottendorfer Mühle	Part II
Berg vor Zwenkau	Part I	Bobenneukirchen	Part I	Boxdorf	Part I, II
Bergwerk	Part II	Bobersen	Part I	Boxdorfer Weinsbergflur	Part II
Bermannsgrün	Part I	Bobershau	Part II	Boxthal	Part I
Bernbruch	Part I, II	Boblitz	Part II	Brabschütz	Part II
Berndorf	Part I	Bochra	Part I	Brambach	Part I
Berndorfer Mühle	Part I	Bocka	Part II	Brand	Part I, II
Bernitzgrün	Part I	Bocka bei Luppa	Part II	Brandis	Part I
Bernsbach	Part I	Bocka	Part I	Brandvorwerk	Part I
Bernsdorf	Part I, II	Bockau	Part I, II	Brantweinhaus	Part I
Bernshäuser	Part II	Bockelwitz	Part I	Bratków	Part II
Bernstadt auf dem Eigen	Part II	Bocken	Part II	Braumühle	Part I
Bernstein	Part II	Bockendorf	Part I	Brauna	Part II
Berntitz bei Staucha	Part II	Bockisches Lehngut	Part I	Braunmühle bei Bernutzgrün	Part I
Berrenth	Part II	Bocksdorf	Part I	Braunsdorf	Part II
Berthelsdorf	Part I, II	Bocksthal	Part I	Bräunsdorf	Part I, II
Bertholdsdorf	Part I	Bockwa	Part I	Braunsdorf bei Tharandt	Part II
Bertsdorf	Part II	Bockwein	Part II	Brauschwitz	Part II
Berutitz bei Mügeln	Part I	Bockwen	Part II	Brausenstein	Part II
Berzdorf	Part II	Bockwitz	Part I, II	Brausswig	Part I
Berzdorf auf dem Eigen	Part II	Boda	Part I	Brautitz	Part II
Bettelmühle	Part I	Boden	Part II	Brechhaus	Part II
Beucha bei Brandis	Part I	Bodenbach	Part II	Brees	Part I
Beucha bei Flössberg	Part I	Boden mit Schindelbach	Part II	Brehmen	Part II
Beutha	Part I	Bodenmühle	Part II	Breiteberg	Part II
Beutig	Part II	Boderitz	Part II	Breite Lehn	Part II
Beyerfeld	Part I	Bodnitz	Part II	Breitenau	Part II
Beyersdorf	Part I	Bogatynia	Part II	Breitenbach	Part II
Białopole	Part II	Böhla	Part II	Breitenberg	Part II
Bieberach	Part I	Böhla bei Ortrandt	Part II	Breitenborn	Part I
Bieberstein	Part II	Böhlau	Part II	Breitenbrunn	Part I
Biedrzychowice Górne	Part II	Böhlen	Part I, II	Breitendorf	Part II
Biehla	Part II	Böhlitz	Part I	Breitenfeld	Part I
Bienenmühle	Part II	Böhmisch	Part II	Breitenhof	Part I
Bienhof	Part II	Böhmisch Bollung	Part II	Breitenstein	Part I
Biensdorf	Part II	Böhmische Folge	Part II	Breitingen	Part I
Biesern	Part I	Bohnitzsch	Part II	Breske	Part II
Binnewitz	Part I, II	Bohra	Part II	Bretmühlen-Revier	Part I
Birkau	Part II	Böhrigen	Part I	Bretnig	Part II
Birkenhain	Part II	Bolbritz	Part II	Brettnig	Part II
Birkenhäuser	Part I	Bonnewitz	Part II	Breunsdorf	Part I
Birkenroda	Part II	Börigen	Part I	Briesing	Part II
Birkigt	Part II	Boritz	Part II	Briesnitz	Part II
Birkigt bei Posseck	Part I	Börkewitz	Part I	Briessnitz	Part II
Birkigt bei Schilbach	Part I	Borlas	Part II	Briestewitz	Part II

KINGDOM OF SAXONY
Parts I and II - Master Index

LOCALITY	PART
Brockau	Part I
Brockwitz	Part II
Brohna	Part II
Bröhsen	Part I
Brokau	Part I
Brösa	Part II
Brösang	Part II
Bröschen	Part II
Broschwitz	Part II
Brosen	Part II
Brösen	Part I
Brösnitz	Part II
Brotenfeld	Part I
Bruchheim	Part I
Bruchschenke	Part II
Brückengut	Part II
Brückenhäuser	Part I
Brüderwiese	Part II
Brünlos	Part II
Brunn bei Auerbach	Part I
Brunn bei Reichenbach	Part I
Brunndöbra	Part I
Brünnelsberg	Part I
Brünnlasberg	Part I
Brünnlastgüter	Part II
Bubendorf	Part I
Buch	Part I
Bucha	Part I
Buchhäuser	Part I
Buchheim	Part I
Buchhöhe	Part I
Buchholz	Part II
Buchholz bei Bocka	Part II
Buchwald	Part I, II
Buchwalda	Part II
Buda	Part II
Budigas	Part I
Bühlau	Part II
Bulleritz	Part II
Burgane	Part I
Burgberg	Part I
Bürgeraue	Part I
Burghausen	Part I
Burgmühle bei Kummersheim	Part I
Burgstädt	Part I
Burgstädtel	Part II
Burgstädtel bei Borthen	Part II
Burgstädtel bei Briessnitz	Part II
Burgstein	Part I
Burk	Part II
Burkartshain	Part I
Bürkau	Part II
Burkersdorf	Part I, II
Burkershain	Part I
Burkhardswalde	Part II
Burkhardtsdorf	Part II
Burkhardtsgrün	Part I
Burkhardtswalde	Part II
Buscheritz	Part II
Buschermühle	Part II
Buschmühle	Part I, II
Buschschenke	Part II
Buschvorwerk	Part II
Butterberg	Part II
Buttergrund	Part I
Buttervorwerk	Part II

LOCALITY	PART
C	
Cainsdorf	Part I
Calbitz	Part I
Calinberg	Part II
Callenberg	Part II
Camenz	Part II
Caminau bei Königswartha	Part II
Caminau bei Radibor	Part II
Cammerhof	Part II
Cämmerrey	Part I
Cämmerswalde	Part II
Canitz bei Meissen	Part II
Canitz bei Oschatz	Part I
Canitz bei Wurzen	Part I
Canitz Christina	Part II
Cannewitz	Part I, II
Cannewitz bei Gröditz	Part II
Cannewitz bei Marienstern	Part II
Carlsberg	Part II
Carlsbrunn	Part II
Carlsdorf	Part I, II
Carlsgaffe	Part I
Carlsruhe	Part II
Carlsrune	Part I
Carolinenhof	Part I
Carolsfeld	Part I
Carpzovische Land	Part I
Carsdorf	Part I
Carthausa	Part I
Carthause	Part I
Casabra	Part I
Caseritz	Part II
Cassabra	Part I
Casslau	Part II
Catharinenberg	Part II
Cauritz	Part II
Cavertitz	Part I
Ceesewitz	Part I
Charlottenhof	Part I
Charlottenruh	Part II
Charthause	Part I
Chemnitz	Part II
Chrieschwitz	Part I
Christgrün	Part I
Christiansreuth	Part I
Christoph	Part I
Churschütz	Part II
Chursdorf	Part I
Clanzschwitz bei Strehla	Part I
Classenbach	Part II
Clausnitz	Part I, II
Clauzschwitz bei Stuchitz	Part I
Clennen	Part I
Cleuden	Part I
Clieben	Part II
Closterberg	Part I
Closterbuch	Part I
Closter Freiheit	Part II
Closter Geringswalde	Part I
Clostergüter	Part I
Clostermühle	Part I, II
Cobenthal	Part II
Coblenz	Part II
Colditz	Part I
Collmen	Part I
Cöllmichen	Part I

LOCALITY	PART
Cöllmsmühle	Part I
Cölln	Part II
Cöllnitz	Part I
Colmnitz	Part II
Colmnitzmühle	Part I
Commerau bei Kauppa	Part II
Commerau bei Königswartha	Part II
Commichau	Part I
Connewitz	Part I
Conradsdorf	Part II
Conradswiese	Part I
Constappel	Part II
Copitz	Part II
Corba	Part I
Cortnitz	Part II
Coschütz	Part I, II
Cosel bei Königsbrück	Part II
Cosel im Gebirge	Part I
Coselitz	Part II
Cossen	Part I
Cossern	Part II
Cosslitz	Part II
Cosswiger Weinbergsgemeinde	Part II
Costewitz	Part I
Coswig	Part II
Cotta	Part II
Cradefeld	Part I
Crandorf	Part I
Cranzahl	Part II
Cränzmühle	Part II
Cratza	Part II
Cratzhammer	Part II
Creilenhain	Part I
Crimmitzschau	Part I
Crinitzleithen	Part I
Cröbern	Part I
Crossen	Part I
Crostau	Part II
Crostewitz	Part I
Crostigall	Part I
Crostwitz	Part II
Crotenlaide	Part II
Crotta	Part II
Crottendorf	Part I, II
Crumbach	Part I
Crumhermsdorf	Part II
Crummenhennersdorf	Part II
Crünitzleithen	Part I
Culitzsch	Part I
Culm	Part I
Culmhäuser	Part I
Culten	Part I
Cunersdorf	Part I, II
Cunertswalde	Part II
Cunewalde	Part II
Cunnersdorf	Part I, II
Cunnersdorf an der Roder	Part II
Cunnersdorf auf dem Eigen	Part II
Cunnersdorf bei Hainichen	Part I
Cunnersdorf bei Helfenberg	Part II
Cunnersdorf bei Hohnstein	Part II
Cunnersdorf bei Kaitz	Part !I
Cunnersdorf bei Kamenz	Part II
Cunnersdorf bei Königstein	Part II
Cunnersdorf bei Lausa	Part II
Cunnersdorf bei Leipzig	Part I
Cunnersdorf bei Pirna	Part II

KINGDOM OF SAXONY
Parts I and II - Master Index

LOCALITY	PART
Dubrau	Part II
Dürnberg	Part I
Dürre Bühlau	Part II
Dürre Fuchs	Part II
Dürre Henne	Part I
Dürrenbach	Part I
Dürrenberg	Part I
Dürrengerbisdorf	Part I
Dürrenuhlsdorf	Part II
Dürrgoseln	Part I
Dürrhennersdorf	Part II
Dürrhof	Part II
Dürr Jessnitz	Part II
Dürrröhrsdorf	Part II
Dürrweitzschen	Part I
Dürrwicknitz	Part II
Dzialoszyn	Part II

E

LOCALITY	PART
Ebelsbrunn	Part I
Ebendörfel	Part II
Ebenheit bei Pirne	Part II
Ebenheit unterm Lilienstein	Part II
Ebersbach	Part I, II
Ebersbachmühle	Part I
Ebersberg	Part I
Ebersbrunn	Part I
Ebersdorf	Part II
Ebersgrün	Part I
Ebertsmühle bei Tirpersdorf	Part I
Ebmath	Part I
Eckartsberg	Part II
Eckersbach	Part I
Eckersberg	Part I, II
Eckersdorf	Part II
Eckertsberg	Part I
Ehrenberg	Part I, II
Ehrenfriedersdorf	Part II
Ehrenzipfel	Part I
Ehrethaus	Part I
Eibenberg	Part II
Eibenstock	Part I
Eich	Part I
Eicha	Part I
Eichardt	Part I
Eichgraben	Part II
Eichhardt	Part I
Eichhäuser	Part I
Eichicht	Part I
Eichigt	Part I
Eichigthäuser	Part I
Eichlaide	Part II
Eichtermühle	Part II
Eingelhardtsgrün	Part I
Einsiedel	Part I, II
Eisenberg	Part II
Eiserode auf dem Eigen	Part II
Eisschenke	Part II
Elbe	Part II
Elbersdorf	Part II
Elbisbach	Part I
Elend	Part II
Elgersdorf	Part II
Ellefeld	Part I
Ellersdorf	Part II
Elm	Part I

LOCALITY	PART
Elster	Part I
Elsterberg	Part I
Elstertrebnitz	Part I
Elstra	Part II
Elterlein	Part II
Elzenberg	Part II
Engelmühle	Part II
Engelsdorf	Part I
Entenschenke	Part II
Eppendorf	Part II
Erbisdorf	Part II
Erbmannsdorf	Part II
Erdmannsdorf	Part II
Erdmannshain	Part I
Erfenschlag	Part II
Erlabrunn	Part I
Erlau	Part I
Erlbach	Part I, II
Erlebach	Part I
Erlenmühle	Part I
Erlhammer	Part I
Erlhäuser	Part I
Erlicht	Part II
Erlichtgut	Part II
Erlichtmühle bei Elstra	Part II
Erlln	Part I
Erlmühle	Part I
Ermendorf	Part II
Ernstthal	Part II
Errlicht	Part II
Eschdorf	Part II
Eschefeld	Part I
Eschenbach	Part I
Eschenbach bei Wolkenstein	Part II
Espenhain	Part I
Espig	Part I
Esse bei Heinersgrün	Part I
Etzdorf	Part I
Etzoldshain	Part I
Euba	Part II
Eubabrunn	Part I
Eubenberg	Part II
Eula	Part I
Eulau	Part I
Euldorf	Part II
Eule	Part II
Eulendorf	Part I
Eulenmühle	Part II
Eulenstein	Part I
Eulitz	Part II
Eulmühle	Part II
Eulowitz	Part II
Eutrich	Part II
Eutritzsch	Part I
Eutschütz	Part II
Eyla	Part I
Eythra	Part I

F

LOCALITY	PART
Fälbach	Part I
Falken	Part II
Falkenau	Part I, II
Falkenbach	Part II
Falkenberg	Part II
Falkenhain	Part I
Falkenhain bei Dohna	Part II

LOCALITY	PART
Falkenhain bei Schmiedeberg	Part II
Falkenhäuser	Part II
Falkenstein	Part I
Fasendorf	Part I
Faule Katze	Part I
Feilerhaus bei Tiefenbrunn	Part I
Feldhaus	Part II
Feldhäuser	Part II
Feldleuba	Part II
Feldschönau	Part II
Feldwiese	Part I
Fernrückerswalde	Part II
Fichte	Part II
Fichtelschenke	Part II
Fichtenhäuser	Part I
Fichtenmühle	Part I
Fichtigsthal	Part I
Fichtzig	Part I
Fickersgrün	Part I
Finkenburg	Part II
Finkenmühle bei Ottenhain	Part I
Finsterau	Part II
Fischbach	Part II
Fischendorf	Part I
Fischergasse bei Meissen	Part II
Fischerhaus	Part I
Fischhaus	Part II
Fischheim	Part I
Fleissig	Part II
Flemmingen	Part I
Flöha	Part II
Flössberg	Part I
Flosslohnhaus bei Görsdorf	Part II
Flossmühle	Part II
Folbern	Part II
Forberg	Part I
Forchheim	Part I
Fördergersdorf	Part II
Förderjessen	Part II
Förstel	Part II
Förstgen	Part I
Forsthaus am Ochsenkopf	Part I
Forsthaus an der Mulde	Part I
Forsthaus an der Wilzsch	Part I
Forsthaus bei der Antonshütte	Part I
Forsthaus bei Eibenstock	Part I
Forsthaus bei Kössern	Part I
Forsthaus bei Langenbernsdorf	Part I
Forsthaus bei Seidewitz	Part I
Forsthaus Grünthal	Part II
Forsthaus Heidelbach	Part II
Forsthaus Kriegwald	Part II
Forstmühle	Part II
Foschenroda	Part I
Franken	Part II
Frankenau	Part I
Frankenberg	Part II
Frankenhausen	Part I
Frankenheim	Part I
Frankenhof	Part I, II
Frankenstein	Part II
Frankenthal	Part II
Franzmühle	Part I
Frauenbach	Part II
Frauendorf	Part I
Frauenhain	Part II
Frauenstein	Part II

KINGDOM OF SAXONY
Parts I and II - Master Index

LOCALITY	PART	LOCALITY	PART	LOCALITY	PART
Fraunbach	Part II	Gaunitz	Part I	Goes	Part II
Fraundorf	Part I	Gaunsgrün	Part I	Goess	Part II
Frauwalda	Part I	Gaussig	Part II	Gohla	Part II
Freiberg	Part I, II	Gaustritz	Part II	Göhlenau	Part II
Freibergsdorf	Part II	Gautzsch	Part I	Gohlis	Part I, II
Freihufe zu Neukirch	Part II	Gävernitz	Part II	Göhlis	Part I
Freikäuser	Part II	Gävernitz	Part II	Göhlis bei Riesa	Part II
Freitelsdorf	Part II	Gebersbach	Part I	Göhra	Part II
Fremdiswalde	Part I	Gebirge	Part II	Göhren	Part I
Friebus	Part I	Geiersberg	Part I, II	Göhrengüter	Part I
Friedebach	Part II	Geiersdorf	Part II	Göhrenz	Part I
Friedeburg	Part II	Geigengrün	Part I	Gohrisch	Part II
Friedelmühle	Part II	Geilsdorf	Part I	Göhrisch	Part II
Friedensthal	Part II	Geising	Part II	Golberode	Part II
Friedersdorf	Part II	Geislitz	Part II	Goldbach	Part II
Friedersdorf bei Reibersdorf	Part II	Geisslitz	Part II	Goldborn	Part I
Friedreich	Part II	Geissmannsdorf	Part II	Goldgrund	Part II
Friedrich	Part II	Geithain	Part I	Goldhausen	Part I
Friedrichsgrün	Part I	Gelenau	Part II	Goldhaussen	Part I
Friedrichstadt	Part II	Gelobtes Land	Part II	Goldhorn	Part I
Friedrichstal	Part II	Georgenfeld	Part II	Goldner Hirsch	Part I
Friedrichsthal	Part I	Georgengrün	Part I	Göldnitz	Part I
Friedrichswalde	Part II	Georgenhammer	Part I	Golk	Part II
Friesen	Part I	Georgenthal	Part I	Göltsche	Part II
Fritzkau	Part II	Georgewitz	Part II	Göltzscheu	Part I
Frohburg	Part I	Geppersdorf	Part II	Golzermühle	Part I
Frohnau	Part II	Gepülzig	Part I	Golzern	Part I
Fuchshain	Part I	Gerichshain	Part I	Golzscha	Part II
Fuchsmühle	Part I	Geringswalde	Part I	Gölzscha	Part II
Fuchspohl	Part I	Gerinswalde	Part II	Gölzschhäuser	Part I
Fuchswinkel	Part I	Gersdorf	Part I, II	Gombsen	Part II
Fürstenau	Part II	Gersdorf bei Hainichen	Part I	Gomlitz	Part II
Fürstenhain	Part II	Gersdorf bei Leisnig	Part I	Gommern	Part II
Fürstenthal	Part II	Gertitzsch	Part II	Gommlitz	Part II
Fürstenwalde	Part II	Gesau	Part II	Gompitz	Part II
Furth	Part II	Geschwitz	Part I	Gönnsdorf	Part II
		Gestewitz	Part I	Gönsdorf	Part II
G		Gettengrün	Part I	Goppeln	Part II
		Geyer	Part II	Goppelsgrün	Part I
Gaatzen	Part I	Gickelshäuser	Part II	Göppersdorf	Part I, II
Gabel	Part II	Giedlitz	Part II	Gopplasgrün	Part I
Gablenz	Part I, II	Gielsberg	Part I	Görbersdorf	Part II
Gadewitz	Part I	Gierth	Part I	Gorisch	Part II
Gahlenz	Part II	Giessenstein	Part II	Göritzhain	Part I
Galgenschenke	Part II	Giessmannsdorf	Part II	Gorknitz	Part II
Gallschutz	Part II	Gilsberg	Part I	Görlitz	Part I
Gallschütz	Part I	Gippe	Part I	Görna	Part II
Gamig	Part II	Gipphäuser	Part I	Gornau	Part II
Ganernitz	Part II	Glashütte	Part II	Gornewitz	Part I
Gansgrün	Part I	Glasten	Part I	Görnitz	Part I
Ganshorn	Part I	Glaubitz	Part II	Gornsdorf	Part II
Gansmühle	Part I	Glaubnitz	Part II	Gorschmitz	Part I
Ganzig	Part I	Glauchau	Part II	Görschnitz	Part I
Gärnitz	Part I	Glauschnitz	Part II	Görsdorf	Part II
Garnsdorf	Part II	Gleina	Part II	Görtitz	Part II
Garsebach	Part II	Gleisberg	Part I, II	Gorusdorf	Part II
Gärtitz	Part I, II	Globenstein	Part I	Görzig	Part I, II
Gaschütz	Part I	Glösa	Part II	Gosau	Part I
Gaschwitz	Part I	Glossen	Part I, II	Gościszów	Part II
Gasern	Part II	Gnandorf	Part I	Gosdorf	Part II
Gassenreuth	Part I	Gnandstein	Part I	Goselitz	Part I
Gässnitz	Part II	Gnaschwitz	Part II	Goseln	Part I
Gastewitz	Part I	Göbeln	Part II	Gospersgrün	Part I
Gatzen	Part I	Göbschelwitz	Part I	Gossberg	Part I
Gaudlitz	Part I	Göda	Part II	Gossdorf	Part II
Gaudlitzschenke	Part I	Gödelitz	Part II	Gosswitz	Part II
Gaulis	Part I	Gödlau	Part II	Gostewitz	Part II

KINGDOM OF SAXONY
Parts I and II - Master Index

LOCALITY	PART	LOCALITY	PART	LOCALITY	PART
Gostritz	Part II	Grossburgk	Part II	Grosssermuth	Part I
Göswein	Part I	Grosscotta	Part II	Grossstädteln	Part I
Göttengrün	Part I	Grossdalzig	Part I	Grossstädten	Part I
Gottesberg	Part I	Grossdehsa	Part II	Grosssteinberg	Part I
Gotteshausgut	Part I	Grossdeuben	Part I	Grossstolpen	Part I
Gottgetreu	Part II	Grossdittmannsdorf	Part II	Gross Storchwitz	Part I
Gotthelffriedrichsgrund	Part II	Grossdobritz	Part II	Grossstorkwitz	Part I
Gottleuba	Part II	Grossdöbschütz	Part II	Grosstrebnitz	Part II
Gottreu	Part II	Grossdölzig	Part I	Grossvoigtsberg	Part II
Gottschdorf	Part II	Grossdorfhain	Part II	Grosswaltersdorf	Part II
Gottscheina	Part I	Grossdrebnitz	Part II	Grossweitschen	Part I
Göttwitz	Part I	Grossdubrau	Part II	Grosswelka	Part II
Gräben im Thal	Part I	Grossenhain	Part II	Grosswetteritzsch	Part I
Grabischau	Part II	Grosserkmannsdorf	Part II	Grosswiederitzsch	Part I
Grabisch Mühle	Part II	Grossförstchen	Part II	Grosswischstauden	Part I
Gräfenhainer-Mühle	Part I	Grossfriesen	Part I	Grosswüstalbertitz	Part II
Grafenhofschenke	Part II	Grossgaussig	Part II	Grosszöbern	Part I
Gränitz	Part II	Grossgrabe	Part II	Grosszössen	Part I
Gränze	Part II	Grossgraupe	Part II	Grosszschachwitz	Part II
Gränzmühle	Part II	Grosshähnchen	Part II	Grosszschepa	Part I, II
Grassdorf	Part I	Grossharthau	Part II	Grosszschocher	Part I
Graumnitz	Part I	Grosshartmannsdorf	Part II	Grottewitz	Part I
Graupzig	Part II	Grosshennersdorf	Part II	Grötzsch	Part II
Grauschütz	Part II	Grosshermsdorf	Part I	Grubditz	Part II
Grauschwitz	Part I	Grossjahna	Part II	Grube	Part II
Grebern	Part II	Grosskagen	Part II	Gruben	Part II
Grechewitz	Part I	Grosskunitz	Part II	Grubnitz	Part I
Grechwitz	Part I	Grosslimmritz	Part I	Grubschütz	Part II
Greenfield	Part II	Grossluga	Part II	Gruhna	Part I
Gregewitz	Part I	Grossmilkau	Part I	Grüllenburg	Part II
Greifendorf	Part I	Grossmiltitz	Part I	Grüllenburger	Part II
Greifenhain	Part I	Grossmühle	Part I	Grumbach	Part I, II
Greissing	Part I	Grossnaundorf	Part II	Grün	Part I
Greissinger Mühle	Part I	Grossockrilla	Part II	Gruna	Part I
Greitzschütz	Part I	Grossoderwitz	Part I	Grüna	Part I, II
Greitzschützher Mühle	Part I	Grossolbersdorf	Part II	Gruna bei Nossen	Part II
Grethen	Part I	Grossölsa	Part II	Grunau	Part II
Greussnig	Part I	Grossopitz	Part II	Grünau	Part II
Greussniger Mühle	Part I	Grosspardau	Part I	Grunau bei Rosswein	Part I
Griesbach	Part I, II	Grosspelsen	Part I	Grünaue	Part II
Griesbachmühle	Part II	Grosspetschau	Part I	Grünbach	Part I
Griessbach	Part II	Grosspöhla	Part I	Grünberg	Part I, II
Grillenburg	Part II	Grosspöhsig	Part I	Grünbusch	Part II
Grimma	Part I	Grossporitzsch	Part II	Grund	Part II
Gröba	Part I	Grosspösna	Part I	Grundau	Part II
Grobau	Part I	Grosspössna	Part I	Grundhäuser	Part II
Grobenmühle	Part I	Grosspostwitz	Part II	Grundmühle	Part I, II
Gröbenmühle	Part I	Grosspötschau	Part I	Grüne Tanne	Part II
Gröbern	Part II	Grossprausitz	Part II	Grünfeld	Part II
Gröblitz	Part I	Grosspresen	Part II	Grüngräbchen	Part II
Gröbschütz	Part I	Grosspriesligk	Part I	Grünhain	Part I
Grödel	Part II	Grossquerbitzsch	Part I	Grünhainichen	Part II
Gröditz	Part II	Grossraschütz	Part II	Grünholz	Part I
Groitzsch	Part I, II	Grossröhrsdorf	Part II	Grünlichtenberg	Part I
Groitzschhäuser	Part I	Grossröhrsdorf bei Pirna	Part II	Grünpöhl	Part I
Gröppendorf	Part I	Grossröhrsdorf bei Radeberg	Part II	Grünrodaer Mühle	Part I
Groptitz	Part I	Grossrückerswalde	Part II	Grünstädtel	Part I
Grossbardau	Part I	Grossrügeln	Part I	Grünthal	Part II
Grossbauchlitz	Part I	Grossrümpf	Part II	Grützemühle	Part II
Grossböhla	Part I	Grösssch	Part I	Gückelsberg	Part II
Grossböhlen	Part I	Grossschirma	Part II	Guhra	Part II
Grossbörnchen	Part II	Grossschlaisdorf	Part I	Güldengossa	Part I
Grossborthen	Part II	Grossschlatitz	Part I	Gundorf	Part I
Grossbothen	Part I	Grossschönau	Part II	Gunnersdorf	Part II
Grossbröhsern	Part II	Grossschweidnitz	Part II	Günsdorf	Part II
Grossbrösern	Part II	Grosssedlitz	Part II	Günthersdorf	Part II
Grossbuch	Part I	Grossseitschen	Part II	Gunzen	Part I

397

KINGDOM OF SAXONY
Parts I and II - Master Index

KINGDOM OF SAXONY
Parts I and II - Master Index

LOCALITY	PART	LOCALITY	PART	LOCALITY	PART
Hinterplenerleithe	Part I	Holzmühlen bei Schöneck	Part I	Jessen bei Okrilla	Part II
Hinterreissig	Part I	Hopfgarten	Part II	Jesseritz	Part II
Hirschbach	Part II	Horka	Part II	Jessnitz	Part I, II
Hirschberg	Part II	Horlasgrün	Part I	Jessritz	Part II
Hirschfeld	Part I, II	Hormersdorf	Part II	Jetscheba	Part II
Hirschfelde	Part I	Hosterwitz	Part I	Jetschoba	Part II
Hirschgrundmühle	Part II	Hübelschenke	Part II	Jiedlitz	Part II
Hirschleitmühle	Part II	Hubertusburg	Part I	Joachimstein	Part II
Hirschmühle	Part I, II	Hühndorf	Part II	Jocketa	Part I
Hirschsprung	Part II	Hundsgrün	Part I	Jocuschberg	Part II
Hirschstein	Part II	Hundshübel	Part I	Johanngeorgenstadt	Part I
Hochhermsdorf	Part I	Hundsnase	Part I	Johannishof	Part II
Hochkirch	Part II	Hünerkopf	Part II	Johannisthal	Part II
Hochweitzschen	Part I	Huth	Part II	Johnsbach	Part II
Höckendorf	Part I, II	Hutha	Part II	Johnsdorf	Part II
Höckericht	Part I	Huthe	Part II	Jöhstadt	Part II
Höckricht	Part I	Hutherleithen	Part I	Jokischberg	Part I
Hof	Part I	Hütten	Part II	Josephidorf	Part II
Höfchen	Part I	Hütten bei Königstein	Part II	Josephsdorf	Part II
Hofehäuser	Part II	Hüttengrund	Part II	Juchheh	Part II
Höfel	Part I	Hüttengrundmühle	Part II	Jüdenberg	Part II
Hofemühle	Part I	Hüttenmühle	Part II	Jüdenhain	Part II
Höfgen	Part I, II	Hüttenschachen	Part I	Jüdenloh	Part I
Hofhainersdorf	Part II				
Höflein	Part I, II	**I**		**K**	
Hoflösnitz	Part II				
Hohburg	Part I	Ibanitz	Part II	Kaditz	Part II
Hohburkersdorf	Part II	Ickowitz	Part II	Kaditzäbschütz	Part II
Hohe Fichte	Part II	Ilkendorf	Part II	Kaditzsch	Part I
Hohehaus	Part I	Ilm	Part I	Kadorf	Part I
Hohekreutz	Part I	Imnitz	Part I	Käferhain	Part I
Hohe Linde	Part II	Ingel	Part I	Kahnsdorf	Part I
Hohendorf	Part I	Ingelsburg	Part I	Kaisitz	Part II
Hoheneck	Part II	Ingelsmühle	Part I	Kaitz	Part II
Hohenfichte	Part II	Irbersdorf	Part II	Kalbitz	Part I
Hohengrün	Part I	Irfersgrün	Part I	Kälderhaus	Part I
Hohenheida	Part I	Irgersdorf	Part II	Kalkgrün	Part I
Hohenkirchen	Part I	Irrgang	Part I	Kalkreuth	Part II
Hohenlauft	Part I			Kaltenborn	Part I
Hohenlinde	Part II	**J**		Kalthausen	Part I
Hohenreuth	Part I			Kaltofen	Part I
Hohenstein	Part II	Jacobsthal	Part II	Kamenz	Part II
Hohentanne	Part II	Jädenhain	Part II	Kandelhof	Part I
Hohenwussen	Part I	Jägerhaus	Part I	Kändler	Part II
Hohkirch	Part II	Jägerhof	Part II	Kanitz	Part II
Hohnbach	Part I	Jägersgrün	Part I	Kappel	Part II
Hohndorf	Part I, II	Jahna	Part I	Kappelmühle	Part II
Hohngut	Part II	Jahnishausen	Part II	Kapsdorf	Part I
Hohnstädt	Part I	Jahnmühle	Part I	Karcha	Part II
Hohnstein	Part II	Jahnsbach	Part II	Karlsfeld	Part I
Hoiersdorf	Part I	Jahnsdorf	Part II	Karnmühle	Part II
Hoiersmühle	Part I	Jahnsgrün	Part I	Karrenmühle bei Rittersberg	Part II
Höl+lenguth	Part II	Jahnshain	Part I	Kaschka	Part II
Höllenmühle	Part II	Jahnshorn	Part I	Kaschwitz	Part II
Höllensteg	Part I	Jähsnitz	Part II	Käseberg	Part II
Höllkruken	Part I	Jänkowitz	Part II	Kastamendörfel	Part II
Höllmühle	Part I	Jannowitz	Part II	Käthewitz	Part II
Hollscha	Part II	Jäschütz	Part II	Katschwitz	Part II
Holsch Dubrau	Part II	Jasna Góra	Part II	Katsdorf	Part I
Holzecke	Part II	Jauer	Part II	Kattnitz	Part I
Hölzelmühle	Part II	Jauernick	Part II	Katzenberg	Part II
Holzhau	Part II	Jeesewitz	Part I	Katzenhäuser	Part II
Holzhausen	Part I	Jenkwitz	Part II	Katzenmühle	Part I
Holzhäuser	Part II	Jensdorf	Part II	Kaufbach	Part II
Holzmühle	Part I	Jerisau	Part II	Kaufungen	Part I
Holzmühle bei Haargrunde	Part I	Jesau	Part II	Kauppa	Part II
Holzmühle bei Tirschendorf	Part I	Jeschütz	Part II	Kauscha	Part II
		Jessen bei Lommatzsch	Part II		

399

KINGDOM OF SAXONY
Parts I and II - Master Index

LOCALITY	PART	LOCALITY	PART	LOCALITY	PART
Kauschwitz	Part I	Kleindorfhain	Part II	Kleinschirma	Part II
Kautzsch	Part II	Kleindrebig	Part II	Kleinschlaisdorf	Part I
Kegel	Part I	Kleindrebnitz	Part II	Kleinschlatitz	Part I
Keilbusch	Part II	Kleindubrau	Part II	Kleinschönau	Part II
Keilbuschhäuser	Part II	Kleinelbersdorf	Part II	Kleinschönberg	Part II
Keilmühle bei Wiedersberg	Part I	Kleinemühle	Part II	Kleinschweidnitz	Part II
Keiselwitz	Part I	Kleinerkmannsdorf	Part II	Kleinseidau	Part II
Kellerhäuser	Part I	Kleinforst	Part I	Kleinseitschen	Part II
Kemmlitz	Part I	Kleinförstchen	Part II	Kleinsiderwitz	Part II
Kemnitz	Part I, II	Kleinfriesen	Part I	Kleinsora	Part II
Kemptau	Part II	Kleingaussig	Part II	Kleinstädteln	Part I
Kerbisdorf	Part II	Kleingeislitz	Part II	Kleinstädten	Part I
Kertzsch	Part II	Kleingera	Part I	Kleinsteinberg	Part I
Kessel bei Adorf	Part I	Kleingieshübel	Part I	Kleinstolpen	Part I
Kessel bei Elster	Part I	Kleingörnitz	Part I	Kleinstorkwitz	Part I
Kesselsdorf	Part II	Kleingraupe	Part II	Kleinstruppen	Part II
Kesselshain	Part I	Kleinhähnchen	Part II	Kleinteichnitz	Part II
Kettewitz	Part II	Klein Hamburg	Part II	Kleintetta	Part II
Ketzergasse	Part II	Kleinharthau	Part II	Kleinthiermig	Part II
Keuern	Part I	Kleinhartmannsdorf	Part II	Kleintrebnitz	Part II
Kiebitz	Part I	Kleinhennersdorf	Part II	Kleinvoigtsberg	Part II
Kiebnitz	Part II	Kleinhermsdorf	Part I	Kleinwaltersdorf	Part II
Kieritzsch	Part I	Kleinhessen	Part I	Kleinweisensand	Part I
Kieschau	Part II	Kleinjänkowitz	Part II	Kleinweitschen	Part I
Kiesdorf auf dem Eigen	Part II	Kleinkagen	Part II	Kleinwelka	Part II
Kieselbach	Part I	Kleinkarsdorf	Part II	Kleinwiederitzsch	Part I
Kindisch	Part II	Kleinkreischa	Part II	Kleinwischstanden	Part I
Kipsdorf	Part II	Kleinkunitz	Part II	Kleinwolmsdorf	Part II
Kirchbach	Part II	Kleinleichnam	Part II	Kleinzöbern	Part I
Kirchberg	Part I, II	Kleinlimbach	Part II	Kleinzössen	Part I
Kitchenblüth	Part I	Kleinlimmritz	Part I	Kleinzschachwitz	Part II
Kittlitz	Part II	Kleinluga	Part II	Kleinzschepa	Part I, II
Kitzscher	Part I	Kleinmilkau	Part I	Kleinzschocher	Part I
Kitzschergut	Part I	Kleinmiltitz	Part I	Kleppisch	Part II
Klappendorf	Part II	Kleinnaundorf	Part II	Klessig	Part II
Klappermühle	Part II	Kleinneuschönberg	Part II	Klinesaubernitz	Part II
Klatenstein	Part II	Kleinneuslitz	Part I	Klinga	Part I
Klatzschmühle	Part II	Kleinockrilla	Part II	Klingenberg	Part II
Kleba	Part II	Kleinoderwitz	Part I	Klingenhain	Part I
Kleebusch	Part II	Kleinolbersdorf	Part II	Klingenhainer Untermühle	Part I
Kleedorf	Part I	Kleinölsa	Part II	Klingenthal	Part I
Kleina	Part II	Kleinopitz	Part II	Klingerstein	Part I
Kleinbardau	Part I	Kleinpardau	Part I	Klippe	Part I
Kleinbauchlitz	Part I	Kleinpelsen	Part I	Klipphausen	Part II
Kleinbautzen	Part II	Kleinpestitz	Part II	Klipphäuser	Part II
Kleinbernsdorf	Part I, II	Kleinpetschau	Part I	Klix	Part II
Kleinboblitz	Part II	Kleinpodelwitz	Part I	Kloschwitz	Part I
Kleinbobritzsch	Part II	Kleinpöhla	Part I	Klostergut	Part II
Kleinböhla	Part I	Kleinpöhsig	Part I	Klosterhäuser	Part II
Kleinbörnchen	Part II	Kleinpomssen	Part I	Klösterlein	Part I
Kleinborthen	Part II	Kleinporitzsch	Part II	Klosterstrasse	Part II
Kleinbothen	Part I	Kleinpösna	Part I	Klötitz	Part I
Kleinbröhsern	Part II	Kleinpostwitz	Part II	Klotzsche	Part II
Kleinburgk	Part II	Kleinpraga	Part II	Kmehlen	Part II
Kleinburkau	Part II	Kleinprausitz	Part II	Knatewitz	Part I
Kleincarsdorf	Part II	Kleinpresen	Part II	Knaumühle	Part II
Kleinchristgrün	Part I	Kleinpriesligk	Part I	Knauthain	Part I
Kleinchursdorf	Part II	Kleinquerbitzsch	Part I	Knautkleeberg	Part I
Kleincosmannsdorf	Part II	Kleinradmeritz	Part II	Knautnaundorf	Part I
Kleincotta	Part II	Kleinragewitz bei Grimma	Part I	Kniegasse	Part I
Kleindalzig	Part I	Kleinraschütz	Part II	Knobelsdorf	Part II
Kleindehsa	Part II	Kleinrennersdorf	Part II	Kobeln	Part II
Kleindeuben	Part I	Kleinröhrsdorf	Part II	Kobelsdorf	Part I
Kleindittmannsdorf	Part II	Kleinrückerswalde	Part II	Kobenthal	Part II
Kleindobritz	Part II	Kleinrügeln	Part I	Kobitzsch	Part II
Kleindöbschütz	Part II	Kleinrümpf	Part II	Kobitzschwalde	Part I
Kleindölzig	Part I	Kleinrussdorf	Part I	Köblitz	Part II

KINGDOM OF SAXONY
Parts I and II - Master Index

LOCALITY	PART	LOCALITY	PART	LOCALITY	PART
Kobschien	Part II	Krappmühle	Part II	in Hüttengrunde	Part II
Kobschütz	Part I	Kratzhammer	Part II	Kuppritz	Part II
Kockisch	Part I	Kratzsch	Part I	Kürbitz	Part I
Kohlau	Part II	Kraumühle	Part II	Kuxleithen	Part I
Kohlmühle	Part II	Krauschütz	Part II	Kynitzsch	Part II
Kohlosdorf	Part II	Krausitz	Part II		
Kohlung	Part II	Krausnitz	Part II	**L**	
Kohlwesa	Part II	Krauswitz	Part II		
Köhra	Part I	Krebes	Part I	Laas	Part I
Kohren	Part I	Krebs	Part II	Läckwitz	Part I
Koitsch	Part II	Kreckwitz	Part II	Lambzig	Part I
Kokisch	Part I	Kreiern	Part II	Lampersdorf	Part I, II
Kolka bei Ossa	Part I	Kreina	Part I	Lampertswalda	Part I, II
Kolkau bei Seelitz	Part I	Kreinitz	Part II	Landesgemeinde	Part I
Kolkwitz	Part II	Kreischa	Part I, II	Landwüst	Part I
Köllmichen	Part I	Kreischerhof	Part II	Langburkersdorf	Part II
Köllsdorf	Part I	Kreissa	Part II	Langeberg	Part I
Kolzschen	Part I	Krepta	Part II	Langebrück	Part II
Kömmlitz	Part I	Kretzscham Rothensehma	Part II	Langenau	Part I
Königsbrück	Part II	Kretzschmar Rothensehma	Part II	Langenbach	Part I
Königsfeld	Part I	Kreudnitz	Part I	Langenberg	Part I, II
Königshain	Part I, II	Kriebethal	Part I	Langenbernsdorf	Part I
Königsmühle	Part II	Kriebstein	Part I	Langenbuch	Part I
Königstein (Festung)	Part II	Kriegberg	Part I	Langenburkersdorf	Part II
Königstein (Stadt)	Part II	Krienitz	Part II	Langenchursdorf	Part II
Königswalde	Part I, II	Kriepitz	Part II	Langenhain	Part I
Königswartha	Part II	Krieschendorf	Part II	Langenhennersdorf	Part II
Koppelsdorf	Part II	Krieschwitz	Part II	Langenhessen	Part I
Kopschin	Part II	Krietzschwitz	Part II	Langenleuba-Oberhain	Part I
Körbigsdorf	Part II	Krinitz	Part II	Langenreinsdorf	Part I
Korbitz	Part II	Krippen	Part II	Langenrinne	Part II
Körlitz	Part I	Kritzschendorf	Part II	Langenstriegis	Part I
Korna	Part I	Krobtitz	Part II	Langenwolmsdorf	Part II
Kornbach	Part I	Krögis	Part II	Langenwolmsdorfer Schäferei	Part II
Kornhain	Part I	Kronförstchen	Part II	Langhennersdorf	Part II
Kornmühle	Part I	Kroptewitz	Part I	Lastau	Part I
Korpitzsch	Part I	Kröstau	Part I	Latzke	Part II
Kosakenscheuke	Part II	Krottendorf	Part II	Lauba	Part II
Koselitz	Part II	Krumbach	Part I	Laubach	Part II
Kospuden	Part I	Krumhermersdorf	Part II	Laubberg	Part I
Kössern	Part I	Krumhermsdorf	Part II	Laubegast	Part II
Kostrzyna	Part II	Krummenhennersdorf	Part II	Lauben bei Weinböhla	Part II
Köthel	Part II	Krummförstchen	Part II	Laucha	Part II
Köthensdorf	Part I	Krzewiha	Part II	Laueckhaus	Part I
Kotitz	Part II	Kubschütz	Part II	Lauenhain	Part I
Kötitz	Part I, II	Kuckau	Part II	Lauenstein	Part II
Kotschbar	Part I	Kuckeland	Part I	Lauer	Part I
Kottengrün	Part I	Kugelmühlen	Part II	Lausa	Part II
Kottenheide	Part I	Kugelreuth	Part I	Lauschka	Part I
Kötteritzsch	Part I	Kühberg	Part II	Lauschwemme	Part I
Köttern	Part I	Kühkrippe	Part I	Lausen	Part I
Kottewitz	Part II	Kühlmühle	Part I	Lausick	Part I
Köttewitz	Part II	Kühnast	Part II	Lausigk	Part I
Kottewitz an der Elbe	Part II	Kühnhaide	Part II	Lauske bei Hochkirch	Part II
Kottewitz bei Strauda	Part II	Kühnitzsch	Part I	Lauske bei Hollscha	Part II
Kottmarhäuser	Part II	Kühren	Part I	Lausnitz	Part II
Kottmarsdorf	Part II	Kuhschnappel	Part II	Laussnitz	Part II
Kottwitz	Part II	Kuhthurm	Part I	Laute	Part II
Köttwitz	Part II	Kulkwitz	Part I	Lautendorf	Part II
Köttwitzsch	Part I	Kumersheim	Part I	Lauter	Part I
Kötzschau	Part II	Kümmelbüchle	Part I	Lauterbach	Part I, II
Kötzsche	Part II	Kümmelhaus	Part I	Lauterhofen	Part I
Kötzschenbroda	Part II	Kumschütz	Part II	Lauterholz	Part I
Kötzschwitz	Part I	Kunadmühle	Part II	Lautitz	Part II
Krakau	Part II	Kunigundenmühle	Part I	Lautzschen	Part II
Kralapp	Part I	Kunnersdorf	Part II	Lawalde	Part II
Krappe	Part II	Kupferhammer	Part II	Leckwitz	Part I, II

KINGDOM OF SAXONY
Parts I and II - Master Index

KINGDOM OF SAXONY
Parts I and II - Master Index

KINGDOM OF SAXONY
Parts I and II - Master Index

LOCALITY	PART	LOCALITY	PART	LOCALITY	PART
Neuschönfels	Part I	Niederdorf	Part II	Niedermühle	Part I
Neusellerhausen	Part I	Niederdorfchemnitz	Part II	Niedermülsen	Part II
Neuseusslitz	Part II	Niederdornhennersdorf	Part II	Niedermuschitz	Part II
Neusorga	Part I	Niederdrehbach	Part II	Niedermuschütz	Part II
Neusorge	Part I, II	Niederebersbach	Part II	Niedernatzschkau	Part II
Neusornzig	Part I	Niederellefeld	Part I	Niedernatzschung	Part II
Neuspreedorf	Part II	Niederelsdorf	Part I	Niederneukirch	
Neuspremberg	Part II	Niedere Sorge	Part I	am Hochwalde	Part II
Neustadt	Part I, II	Niedereula	Part II	Niederneuschönberg	Part II
Neustädtel	Part I, II	Niedereulowitz	Part II	Niederolbersdorf	Part II
Neustädtel bei Schneeberg	Part I	Niederfähre	Part II	Niederoppach	Part II
Neustadt in Sachsen	Part II	Niederfedlitz	Part II	Niederottendorf	Part II
Neustruppen	Part II	Niederfehra	Part II	Niederottenhain	Part II
Neustützengrün	Part I	Niederforchheim	Part II	Niederpesterwitz	Part II
Neutanbenheim	Part I	Niederfrankenhain	Part I	Niederpfannenstiel	Part I
Neutanneberg	Part II	Niederfraundorf	Part II	Niederpickenhain	Part I
Neutaubenheim	Part II	Niederfriedersdorf	Part II	Niederplanitz	Part I
Neutzsch	Part I	Niederfrohna	Part I	Niederpöbel	Part II
Neuvorwerk	Part I	Niedergarnsdorf	Part II	Niederpoiritz	Part II
Neuwalde	Part II	Niedergersdorf	Part II	Niederpolenz	Part II
Neuwallwitz	Part I	Niederglobenstein	Part I	Niederposta	Part II
Neuwaltersdorf	Part II	Niedergohlis	Part II	Niederpoyritz	Part II
Neuwarnsdorf	Part II	Nieder Goseln	Part I	Niederpretzschendorf	Part II
Neuweissig	Part II	Niedergräfenhain	Part I, II	Niederputzkau	Part II
Neuwelt	Part I	Niedergrauschwitz	Part I	Niederrabenstein	Part II
Neuwerder	Part I	Niedergrumbach	Part II	Niederrathen	Part I
Neuwernsdorf	Part II	Niedergruna	Part II	Niederrauschütz	Part I
Neuwiese	Part II	Niedergrünberg	Part I	Niederreichstädt	Part II
Neuwunschwitz	Part II	Niedergurig	Part II	Niederreinhardtsgrimma	Part II
Neuzaschendorf	Part II	Niederhartmannsbach	Part II	Niederreinsberg	Part II
Neuzinnwald	Part II	Niederhaselbach	Part I, II	Niederrennersdorf	Part II
Nichtewitz	Part I	Niederhäselich	Part II	Niederrochwitz	Part II
Nichzenhain	Part I	Niederhasslau	Part I	Niederrödern	Part II
Nickeritz	Part II	Niederhelmsdorf	Part II	Niederroderwitz	Part II
Nickern	Part II	Niederhermersdorf	Part II	Niederrossau	Part I
Nickolschwitz	Part I	Nieder Herwigsdorf	Part II	Niederruppersdorf	Part II
Nickolsmühle	Part II	Niederhesslitch	Part II	Niedersaida	Part II
Nickritz	Part II	Niederhohndorf	Part I	Niederschindelbach	Part II
Nicolaimühle	Part II	Niederingel	Part I	Niederschindmaas	Part I
Nicollschwitz	Part I	Niederjahna	Part II	Niederschlag	Part II
Nicolsdorf	Part II	Niederjahnsbach	Part II	Niederschlema	Part I
Niebra	Part I	Niederjohnsbach	Part II	Niederschmiedeberg	Part II
Nieda	Part II	Niederkaina	Part II	Niederschmölen	Part I
Niederaffalter	Part I	Niederkemnitz	Part II	Niederschmölln	Part I, II
Niederailsdorf	Part I	Niederkeyna	Part II	Niederschöna	Part II
Niederalbersdorf	Part I	Niederkiesdorf	Part II	Niederschönbach	Part II
Niederalbertsdorf	Part I	Niederkittlitz	Part II	Niederseida	Part II
Niederarnsdorf	Part II	Niederkotitz	Part II	Niederseidewitz	Part II
Niederau	Part II	Niederkrauschwitz	Part I	Niederseifenbach	Part II
Niederauerbach	Part I	Niederkreischa	Part II	Niederseyffenbach	Part II
Nieder Auerswalde	Part II	Niederlangenau	Part II	Niedersohlan an der Spree	Part II
Niederbeiersdorf	Part II	Niederlauba	Part II	Niedersohland am Rotstein	Part II
Niederbelbitz	Part II	Niederlauterstein	Part I	Niederspaar	Part II
Niederberthelsdorf	Part II	Niederlawalde	Part II	Niederspremberg	Part II
Niederbischdorf	Part II	Niederleuba	Part II	Niederstaucha	Part II
Niederbobritzsch	Part II	Niederleutersdorf	Part II	Niedersteina	Part I, II
Niederboiritz	Part II	Niederlichtenau	Part II	Niedersteinbach	Part I
Niederburka	Part II	Niederlockwitz	Part II	Niedersteinpleis	Part I
Niederburkau	Part II	Niederlössnitz	Part I, II	Niederstrahwalde	Part II
Niederburkersdorf	Part II	Niederlungwitz	Part II	Niederstriegis	Part I
Niedercainsdorf	Part I	Niederlützschera	Part I	Niedertaubenheim	Part II
Niedercolmnitz	Part II	Niedermalschwitz	Part II	Niederthalheim	Part I
Niedercrinitz	Part I	Niedermalter	Part II	Niedertoppschedel	Part II
Niedercrossen	Part I	Niedermarbach	Part I	Niederuhna	Part II
Niedercrostau	Part II	Niedermeusegast	Part II	Niederulbersdorf	Part II
Niedercunewalde	Part II	Niedermosel	Part I	Niedervogelsang	Part II
Niedercunnersdorf	Part II	Niedermühlbach	Part II	Niedervoigtsdorf	Part II

KINGDOM OF SAXONY
Parts I and II - Master Index

LOCALITY	PART	LOCALITY	PART	LOCALITY	PART
Niederwanscha	Part II	Oberburkau	Part II	Oberkotitz	Part II
Niederwartha	Part II	Oberburkersdorf	Part II	Oberkreischa	Part II
Niederweigsdorf	Part II	Obercainsdorf	Part I	Oberlangenau	Part II
Niederwiesa	Part II	Obercolmnitz	Part II	Oberlauba	Part II
Niederwinkel	Part II	Obercrinitz	Part I	Oberlauterbach	Part I
Niederwolmsdorf	Part II	Obercrossen	Part I	Oberlawalde	Part II
Niederwürschnitz	Part II	Obercrostau	Part II	Oberleuba	Part II
Niederwutzschwitz	Part I	Obercunewalde	Part II	Oberleutersdorf	Part II
Niederzschanitz	Part II	Obercunnersdorf	Part II	Oberlichtenau	Part II
Niederzschocken	Part I	Oberdöhlen	Part II	Oberlimbach	Part I
Niederzschörnewitz	Part I	Oberdorf	Part II	Oberlockwitz	Part II
Niederzwönitz	Part II	Oberdorfchemnitz	Part II	Oberlommatzsch	Part II
Niedów	Part II	Oberdornhennersdorf	Part II	Oberlosa	Part I
Niegerode	Part II	Oberdrehbach	Part II	Oberlössnitz	Part II
Nieschütz	Part II	Oberebersbach	Part II	Oberlöwenhain	Part II
Niesendorf	Part II	Oberellefeld	Part I	Oberlungwitz	Part II
Nieska	Part II	Oberelsdorf	Part I	Oberlützschera	Part I
Niethen	Part II	Obere Sorge	Part I	Obermalschwitz	Part II
Niethener Mühle	Part II	Obereula	Part II	Obermalter	Part II
Nimbschen	Part I	Obereulowitz	Part II	Obermarbach	Part I
Nimschütz	Part II	Oberforchheim	Part II	Obermarxgrün	Part I
Nimtitz	Part II	Oberförstchen	Part II	Obermeisa	Part II
Nimtschen	Part I	Oberfranken	Part I	Obermeusegast	Part II
Ninive	Part II	Oberfrankenhain	Part I	Obermosel	Part I
Nischütz	Part II	Oberfraundorf	Part II	Obermühlbach	Part II
Nischwitz	Part I	Oberfrohna	Part II	Obermühle	Part I
Nitzschenmühle	Part I	Obergarnsdorf	Part II	Obermuschitz	Part II
Nitzschwitz	Part I	Obergersdorf	Part II	Obermylau	Part I
Nixenhain	Part I	Oberglobenstein	Part I	Obernatzschkau	Part II
Nöbeln	Part I	Obergohlis	Part II	Obernatzschung	Part II
Nödaschütz	Part II	Obergöltzsch	Part I	Obernaundorf	Part II
Nonneholz	Part I	Obergorbitz	Part II	Oberndorf	Part II
Noschkowitz	Part I	Obergoseln	Part I	Oberneudorf	Part I
Noselitz	Part II	Obergräfen	Part I	Oberneukirch am Hochwalde	Part II
Nossen	Part II	Obergräfenhain	Part I, II	Oberneumark	Part I
Nössge	Part II	Obergrauschwitz	Part I	Oberneundorf	Part I
Nössige	Part II	Obergrumbach	Part II	Oberneuschönberg	Part II
Nosslitz	Part II	Obergruna	Part II	Obernitzschka	Part I
Nosswitz	Part I	Obergrünberg	Part I	Oberoderwitz	Part II
Nostitz	Part II	Obergurig	Part II	Oberolbersdorf	Part II
Nöthnitz	Part I, II	Obergurk	Part II	Oberoppach	Part II
Nöthschütz	Part I	Obergurkau	Part II	Oberottendorf	Part II
Nötschütz	Part I	Oberhainsdorf	Part I	Oberottenhain	Part II
Nucknitz	Part II	Oberhartmannsbach	Part II	Oberpesterwitz	Part II
Nüncheritz	Part II	Oberhaselbach	Part I, II	Oberpfannenstiel	Part I
Nünchritz	Part II	Oberhasslau	Part I	Oberpickenhain	Part I
Nundörfel	Part II	Oberhässlich	Part II	Oberpirk	Part I
Nutzung	Part II	Oberheinsdorf	Part I	Oberplanitz	Part I
		Oberhelmsdorf	Part II	Oberpoiritz	Part II
O		Oberhermersdorf	Part II	Oberpolenz	Part II
		Oberhermsdorf	Part II	Oberposta	Part II
Oberaffalter	Part I	Oberhermsgrün	Part I	Oberpoyritz	Part II
Oberalbersdorf	Part I	Oberherwigsdorf	Part II	Oberpretzschendorf	Part II
Oberalbertsdorf	Part I	Oberherwigsdorf bei Zittau	Part II	Oberputzkau	Part II
Oberau	Part II	Oberhesslich	Part II	Oberrabenstein	Part II
Oberauerswalde	Part II	Oberhohndorf	Part I	Oberrannschütz	Part I
Oberaylsdorf	Part I	Oberhütte	Part II	Oberrathen	Part II
Oberbahra	Part II	Oberingel	Part I	Oberrauschenthal	Part I
Oberbeiersdorf	Part II	Oberjahna	Part II	Oberreichenau	Part I
Oberbelbitz	Part II	Oberjohnsbach	Part II	Oberreichenbach	Part I, II
Oberbergen	Part I	Oberkaina	Part II	Oberreichstädt	Part II
Oberberthelsdorf	Part II	Oberkarsdorf	Part I	Oberreinhardtsgrimma	Part II
Oberbischdorf	Part II	Oberkeina	Part II	Oberreinsberg	Part II
Oberblauengrün	Part I	Oberkemnitz	Part II	Oberrennersdorf	Part II
Oberbobritzsch	Part II	Oberkiesdorf	Part II	Oberreussen	Part I
Oberböhlen	Part I	Oberkittlitz	Part II	Oberrittersgrün	Part I
Oberboiritz	Part II	Oberklingenthal	Part I	Oberrochwitz	Part II

KINGDOM OF SAXONY
Parts I and II - Master Index

LOCALITY	PART	LOCALITY	PART	LOCALITY	PART
Oberrödern	Part II	Obverpöbel	Part II	Pammlersmühle	Part I
Oberrodersdorf	Part I	Ochsensaal	Part I	Pamplersmühle	Part I
Oberrossau	Part I	Ockerwitz	Part II	Panisdorf	Part II
Oberrothenbach	Part I	Ockrilla	Part II	Panishain	Part II
Oberruppersdorf	Part II	Ockritz	Part I	Panitz	Part I
Obersachsenberg	Part I	Oderwitz	Part I	Panitzsch	Part I
Obersachsenfeld	Part I	Oebertitz	Part I	Pannewitz am Taucher	Part II
Obersaida	Part II	Oederan	Part II	Pannewitz bei Weidlitz	Part I
Oberschaar	Part II	Oehlisch	Part II	Pappendorf	Part I
Oberscheibe	Part II	Oehna	Part II	Pappenheim	Part I
Oberscheube	Part II	Oelisch	Part II	Papperitz	Part II
Oberschindelbach	Part II	Oellschütz	Part I	Papsdorf	Part I
Oberschindmaas	Part II	Oelsa	Part II	Papstdorf	Part I, II
Oberschlema	Part I	Oelschütz	Part I	Parostensa	Part II
Oberschloditz	Part I	Oelsen	Part II	Paschkowitz	Part I
Oberschlottewitz	Part II	Oelsengrund	Part II	Passditz	Part II
Oberschmiedeberg	Part II	Oelsitz	Part II	Passlermühle	Part I
Oberschmölln	Part II	Oelsnitz	Part I, II	Pasternik	Part II
Oberschöna	Part II	Oelzschau	Part I	Pastmühle	Part I
Oberschönbach	Part II	Oertelsdorf	Part II	Pathen	Part II
Oberseida	Part II	Oertelshain	Part II	Pattersleben	Part II
Oberseidewitz	Part II	Oesse	Part I	Pauitzmühle	Part I
Oberseifenbach	Part II	Oetzsch	Part I	Paulsmühle	Part II
Oberseifersdorf	Part II	Ohorn	Part II	Paunsdorf	Part I
Oberseiffenbach	Part II	Okrilla	Part I	Pausa	Part I
Obersohland am Rotstein	Part II	Olbernhau	Part II	Pauschütz	Part II
Obersohland an der Spree	Part II	Olbersdorf	Part II	Pauschwitz	Part I, II
Oberspaar	Part II	Olganitz	Part I	Pausdorf	Part I
Oberspremberg	Part II	Omsewitz	Part II	Pausitz	Part I, II
Oberstaucha	Part II	Opolno Zdrój	Part II	Pautzsch	Part I
Obersteina	Part I, II	Oppach	Part II	Pautzschmühle	Part I
Obersteinbach	Part I, II	Oppeln	Part II	Pechseifen	Part I
Obersteinpleis	Part I	Oppelsdorf	Part II	Pechtelsgrün	Part I
Oberstötzwitz	Part II	Oppitz	Part II	Pegau	Part I
Oberstrahwalde	Part II	Oppitzsch	Part I	Pegenau	Part II
Oberstützengrün	Part I	Ortelsdorf	Part II	Peintenmühle	Part I
Obertaubenheim	Part II	Ortmannsdorf	Part I	Pelzmühle	Part I, II
Oberthalheim	Part I	Oschatz	Part I	Pelzmusche	Part II
Obertitz	Part I	Ossa	Part I	Penig	Part I
Obertoppschedel	Part II	Osseck	Part I	Penna	Part I
Obertriebel	Part I	Ossel	Part II	Pennrich	Part II
Obertriebelbach	Part I	Ossig	Part I	Penzelmühle	Part I
Oberuhna	Part II	Ossling	Part II	Perba	Part II
Oberulbersdorf	Part II	Ostra	Part II	Peres	Part I
Oberullersdorf	Part II	Ostrau	Part I, II	Perglas	Part I
Obervogelgesang	Part II	Ostritz	Part II	Peritz	Part II
Obervoigtsdorf	Part II	Ostro	Part II	Perne	Part II
Oberwanscha	Part II	Ottenbach	Part II	Peschelmühle	Part II
Oberwartha	Part II	Ottendorf	Part I, II	Peschen	Part II
Oberweigsdorf	Part II	Ottengrün	Part I	Pesterwitz	Part II
Oberweischlitz	Part I	Ottenhain	Part I	Petersbach	Part II
Oberweissig	Part II	Ottenstein	Part I	Petersberg	Part II
Oberwiehra	Part II	Otterhaus bei Plauschwitz	Part I	Petershain	Part II
Oberwiera	Part II	Otterschütz	Part II	Pethau	Part II
Oberwiesa	Part II	Otterwisch	Part I	Petzoldshäuser	Part I
Oberwiesenthal	Part II	Ottowalde	Part II	Petzscher Mark	Part I
Oberwinkel	Part II	Otzdorf	Part I	Petzschwitz	Part II
Oberwirschnitz	Part I	Oybin	Part II	Pfaffenberg	Part I
Oberwolmsdorf	Part II			Pfaffendorf	Part I, II
Oberwürschnitz	Part II	**P**		Pfaffengrün	Part I
Oberwutzschwitz	Part I			Pfaffenhaus	Part I
Oberwyhra	Part II	Pabstdorf	Part II	Pfaffenmühle	Part I
Oberzehren	Part II	Pabstleithen	Part I	Pfaffroda	Part II
Oberzschanitz	Part II	Pabstmühle	Part I	Pfannenhaus	Part I
Oberzschocken	Part I	Pahnitz	Part I	Pfannenkuchenmühle	Part I
Oberzschörnewitz	Part I	Pahrenz	Part II	Pfannenstiel	Part I
Oberzwoka	Part I	Paltzschen	Part II	Pfarrmühle	Part I

KINGDOM OF SAXONY
Parts I and II - Master Index

KINGDOM OF SAXONY
Parts I and II - Master Index

LOCALITY	PART	LOCALITY	PART	LOCALITY	PART
Rammoldsreuth	Part I	Reinberg	Part II	Rockau	Part II
Ramsdorf	Part I	Reinersdorf	Part II	Röcknitz	Part I
Randeck	Part II	Reinhardtsdorf	Part II	Röda	Part I
Rangmühle	Part I	Reinhardtsgrimma	Part II	Roda bei Frohburg	Part I
Rappenberg	Part I	Reinhardtsgrün	Part I	Roda bei Hain	Part II
Räsa	Part II	Reinhardtsthal	Part I	Roda bei Mutzschen	Part I
Raschau	Part I, II	Reinhardtswalde	Part I	Rodau	Part I
Raschütz	Part I	Reinholdshain	Part II	Rödchen	Part I
Raschwitz	Part I	Reinitz	Part II	Rödelmühle	Part I
Rasslitz	Part II	Reinmersgrün	Part I	Röderau	Part II
Rathen	Part II	Reinsdorf	Part I	Röderbrunn	Part II
Rathendorf	Part I	Reinsdorf bei Waldheim	Part I	Rödern	Part II
Rathewalde	Part II	Reinsdorf bei Werdau	Part I	Rodersdorf	Part I
Rathmannsdorf	Part II	Reisewitz	Part II	Rodewisch	Part I
Rattwitz	Part II	Reissig	Part I	Rodewitz bei Crostau	Part II
Raube	Part II	Reissigmühle	Part II	Rodewitz bei Hochkirch	Part II
Rauenstein	Part II	Reitzendorf	Part II	Rödgen	Part I
Rauenthal	Part II	Reitzenhain	Part I, II	Rodlera	Part I
Raufpach	Part I	Remissen	Part II	Rödlitz	Part II
Raum	Part I, II	Rempesgrün	Part I	Rohna	Part II
Raumfeld	Part I	Remsa	Part I	Rohnau	Part II
Raummühle	Part II	Remse	Part II	Rohrbach	Part I, II
Raun	Part I	Remtengrün	Part I	Röhrsdorf	Part II
Rauergrund	Part I	Rennersdorf bei Stolpen	Part II	Roitzsch bei Dresden	Part II
Raunerhammer	Part I	Rennersdorf bei Wilsdruf	Part II	Roitzsch bei Oschatz	Part I, II
Raupenhain	Part I	Reppen	Part I	Roitzsch bei Wurzen	Part I
Rauschenbach	Part II	Reppina	Part II	Roitzschberg	Part II
Rauschenthal	Part I	Reppis	Part II	Roitzschen	Part II
Rauschwitz	Part II	Reppnitz	Part II	Roitzschwiese	Part II
Rausslitz	Part II	Reuckersdorf	Part II	Röllingshain	Part I
Rebersreuth	Part I	Reudnitz	Part I	Rollmühle	Part I
Rebesbrunn	Part I	Reusa	Part I	Romerei	Part II
Rebesgrün	Part I	Reuterhaus	Part II	Römersgrün	Part I
Rechau	Part I	Reuth	Part I	Ronaw	Part II
Rechenberg	Part II	Reuth bei Elster	Part I	Röschen	Part II
Rechenhaus	Part I	Reuth bei Elsterberg	Part I	Rosenberg	Part I
Reckwitz	Part I	Reuth bei Plauen	Part I	Rosenhain	Part II
Rectormühle	Part II	Reuthhäser	Part I	Rösenmühle	Part I
Redemitz	Part I	Reutnitz	Part II	Rosenthal	Part I, II
Regis	Part I	Reutnitzhäser	Part I	Rosentitz	Part II
Rehbach	Part I	Reutschmühle	Part I	Rösschen	Part I
Rehefeld	Part II	Rhäsa	Part II	Rossendorf	Part II
Rehfeld	Part II	Rhensdorf	Part II	Rössnitz	Part I
Rehhübel	Part I	Richtermühle	Part II	Rossthal	Part II
Rehnsdorf	Part II	Richzenhain	Part I	Rosswein	Part I
Reibersdorf	Part II	Riechberg	Part I	Rostig	Part II
Reiboldsgrün	Part I	Riedelmühle	Part I	Rötha	Part I
Reiboldsruhe	Part I	Riekisch	Part I	Rothenbach	Part II
Reichbach	Part II	Riemsdorf	Part II	Röthenbach	Part I, II
Reichenau	Part II	Riesa	Part II	Rothenfurth	Part II
Reichenbach	Part I, II	Rieschen	Part II	Rothenhammer bei Rittersgrün	Part I
Reichenbach bei Hohenstein	Part II	Rietzmar	Part I	Rothenhammer bei Wiesenthal	Part II
Reichenbach bei Langenhennersdorf	Part II	Ringenhain	Part II	Rothenkirchen	Part I
Reichenbach bei Scharfenberg	Part II	Ringenthal	Part I	Röthenmühle	Part I
		Ringethal	Part I	Rothenthal	Part II
Reichenbach bei Waldheim	Part I	Rinnmühle	Part I	Rothersdorf	Part I
Reichenberg	Part II	Rippien	Part II	Röthgen	Part I
Reichenbrand	Part II	Rissbrück	Part I	Röthigen	Part I
Reichenhain	Part II	Rissbrücke	Part I	Rothnauslig	Part II
Reichenheim	Part II	Rittersberg	Part II	Rothschönberg	Part II
Reichersdorf	Part I	Rittmitz	Part I	Rothwernsdorf	Part II
Reichstädt	Part II	Ritzmar	Part I	Rottewitz	Part II
Reichstein	Part II	Robschütz	Part II	Röttis	Part I
Reick	Part II	Rochlitz	Part I	Rottluf	Part II
Reifland	Part II	Rochsburg	Part I	Rottmannsdorf	Part I
Reimtengrün	Part I	Rochsthain	Part I	Rottwerndorf	Part II
		Rochzahn	Part I	Rotzschau	Part I

KINGDOM OF SAXONY
Parts I and II - Master Index

LOCALITY	PART	LOCALITY	PART	LOCALITY	PART
Rubelschütz	Part II	Salzmeste	Part I	Schirgiswalde	Part II
Rüben	Part I	Sand	Part II	Schirrmühle	Part I
Rübenau	Part II	Sandleite	Part I	Schittermühle	Part I
Rückenhain	Part II	Sankt Christoph	Part I	Schkoplau	Part I
Rückersdorf	Part II	Sankt Egidien	Part II	Schkorditz	Part I
Rückerswalde	Part I	Sankt Michaelis	Part II	Schkortitz	Part I
Rückisch	Part I	Sankt Peter	Part I	Schlagewitz	Part I
Rückmarsdorf	Part I	Sankt Thekla	Part I	Schlagwitz	Part I
Rudelsdorf	Part I	Särchen	Part II	Schlaisdorf	Part I
Rudelswalde	Part I	Saritzsch	Part II	Schlanzschweitz	Part I
Ruderitz	Part I	Särka	Part II	Schlauschwitz	Part I
Rüdigsdorf	Part I	Satzung	Part II	Schleben	Part I
Rudolphsdorf	Part II	Saubach	Part I	Schleenhain	Part I
Rudolphsmühle	Part II	Saubachhäuser	Part I	Schlegel	Part I, II
Rugiswalde	Part II	Saugrabenschenke	Part I	Schlehenhain	Part I
Ruhethal	Part II	Saultitz	Part II	Schleinitz	Part II
Ruhhäuser	Part I	Saumühle	Part I	Schletta	Part II
Rümpf	Part II	Saupersdorf	Part I	Schlettau	Part II
Ruppendorf	Part II	Saupsdorf	Part II	Schlettemühle	Part II
Ruppersdorf	Part I	Säuritz	Part II	Schlettheim	Part II
Ruppertsgrün	Part I	Saxdorf	Part II	Schleussig	Part I
Rusdorf	Part II	Sayda	Part II	Schliefermühle	Part II
Rüsdorf	Part II	Schaafhäuser	Part I	Schloditz	Part I
Russdorf	Part II	Schaarhammer	Part I	Schlögelmühle	Part I
Rüssdorf	Part II	Schaddel	Part I	Schloss Chemnitz	Part II
Rüsseina	Part II	Schadendeck	Part I	Schlösschen	Part II
Rüssen	Part I	Schafflegen	Part II	Schlössel	Part II
Russhütte	Part I	Schäller	Part II	Schlösselmühle	Part II
Rützengrün	Part I	Schandau	Part II	Schlossgemeinde	Part I
Rüx	Part I	Schänitz bei Riesa	Part II	Schlosshäuser	Part I
Rybarzowice	Part II	Schänitz bei Schleinitz	Part II	Schlossmühle	Part I, II
		Schanzenmühle	Part I	Schlotterhartha	Part I
S		Scharfenberg	Part II	Schlottwitz	Part II
		Scharfenstein	Part II	Schlottwitzer	Part II
Saalbach	Part I	Scharre	Part II	Schlottwitzer Hütten	Part II
Saalendorf	Part II	Schaudorf	Part II	Schlungwitz	Part II
Saalhausen	Part I, II	Scheckichtmühle	Part II	Schlunzig	Part II
Saalig	Part I	Scheckwitz	Part II	Schmalbach	Part I
Saasdorf	Part I	Schedewitz	Part I	Schmalzgrube	Part II
Sacherhaus	Part I	Schedlichsberg	Part I	Schmannewitz	Part I
Sachsdorf	Part II	Scheerau	Part II	Schmeckwitz	Part II
Sachsenburg	Part II	Scheergrund	Part I	Schmerlitz	Part II
Sachsendorf	Part I	Scheibe	Part II	Schmerzingscher Hammer	Part I
Sachsenfeld	Part I	Scheibe bei Frohnau	Part II	Schmiedeberg	Part II
Sachsengrund	Part I	Scheibe bei Schönbrunn	Part II	Schmiedefeld	Part II
Sachsengütel	Part I	Scheibenberg	Part II	Schmiedewalde	Part II
Sachsenhof	Part II	Scheibengut	Part I	Schmilka	Part II
Sachsgrün	Part I	Scheibenknock	Part I	Schmochtitz	Part II
Sächsische Reuter	Part II	Scheibenmühle	Part II	Schmohla	Part II
Sachsmüuhle	Part II	Scheidebach	Part II	Schmole	Part II
Sachswitz	Part I	Scheidenbach	Part II	Schmölen	Part I
Sacka	Part II	Schellenberg	Part II	Schmölln	Part II
Sackhaus	Part I	Schellerhau	Part II	Schmorditz	Part I
Sadisdorf	Part II	Schellermühle	Part II	Schmorkau	Part I, II
Sageritz	Part II	Schenkhäuser	Part I	Schmörlitz	Part II
Sahlassau	Part I	Scherau	Part II	Schmorren	Part I
Sahlendorf	Part II	Scherfmühle	Part II	Schmorsdorf	Part II
Sahlis	Part I	Schickemühle	Part I	Schnandertrebenitz	Part I
Saida	Part II	Schickenmühle	Part II	Schnarrtanne	Part I
Saigerhütte Grünthal	Part II	Schiedel	Part I	Schneckengrün	Part I
Salbitz	Part I	Schiefermühle	Part II	Schneeberg	Part I
Salga	Part II	Schieritz	Part II	Schneidenbach	Part I
Salhausen	Part II	Schiffermühle	Part I	Schneppendorf	Part I
Salzbach	Part I	Schilbach	Part I	Schodenmühle	Part I
Salzbrunn	Part I	Schilfmühle	Part I	Scholas	Part I
Salzenforst	Part II	Schindelbach	Part II	Scholis	Part I
Salzforstchen	Part II	Schinkenmühle	Part I	Schomerberg	Part I

KINGDOM OF SAXONY
Parts I and II - Master Index

LOCALITY	PART	LOCALITY	PART	LOCALITY	PART
Schöna	Part I, II	Sebenisch	Part I	Sieglitz bei Meissen	Part II
Schönau	Part I, II	Sebnitz	Part II	Siegmar	Part II
Schönau auf dem Eigen	Part II	Sebschütz	Part II	Siehdichfür	Part I
Schönau bei Kamenz	Part II	Seebenisch	Part I	Silbergrube	Part II
Schönbach	Part I, II	Seebitzschen	Part I	Silberstrasse	Part I
Schönberg	Part I, II	Seebschütz	Part II	Singwitz	Part II
Schönborn	Part II	Seegeritz	Part I	Sinkwitz	Part II
Schönbörnchen	Part II	Seehausen	Part I	Sitten	Part I
Schönbörngen	Part II	Seeligstadt	Part II	Skala	Part II
Schönbrunn	Part II	Seelingstadt	Part II	Skassa	Part II
Schönbrunn bei Dresden	Part II	Seelingstädt	Part I	Skässchen	Part II
Schönbrunn bei Grosshennersdorf	Part II	Seelitz	Part I	Skässgen	Part II
Schönbrunn bei Oelsnitz	Part I	Seerhausen	Part I	Skasske	Part II
Schönbrunn bei Radeberg	Part II	Seftewitz	Part I	Skaup	Part II
Schönbrunn bei Treuen	Part I	Sehlis	Part I	Skoplau	Part I
Schönbrunn zum Dresden	Part II	Sehlitz	Part I	Söbitzschen	Part I
Schöneck	Part I	Sehma	Part II	Sobrigau	Part II
Schönecker Waldgemeinde	Part I	Seida	Part II	Söbrigen	Part II
Schönefeld	Part I	Seidau	Part II	Soeulahora	Part II
Schönerstadt	Part II	Seidewitz	Part I	Sohl	Part I
Schönerstädt	Part I	Seidichen	Part II	Söhnitz	Part II
Schönfeld	Part I, II	Seidnitz	Part II	Sohra	Part II
Schönfels	Part I	Seifen	Part II	Sollschwitz	Part II
Schönheide	Part I	Seiferitz	Part II	Sommerau	Part II
Schönheider Hammer	Part I	Seifersbach	Part I	Sommerfeld	Part I
Schönlind	Part I	Seifersdorf	Part II	Sommerluga	Part II
Schönnbrunn bei Wolkenstein	Part II	Seifersdorf bei Dippoldiswalde	Part II	Sömnitz	Part I
Schönnerstädt	Part I	Seifersdorf bei Freiberg	Part II	Somsdorf	Part II
Schönnewitz	Part I, II	Seifersdorf bei Geithain	Part I	Sönitz	Part II
Schottenmühle	Part I	Seifersdorf bei Leisnig	Part I	Sonne Gottes	Part I
Schrebitz bei Nossen	Part II	Seifersdorf bei Rosswein	Part I	Sonnenberg	Part I, II
Schrebitz bei Oschatz	Part I	Seifertshain	Part I	Sonnenmühle bei Oellschütz	Part I
Schreiersgrün	Part I	Seiffen	Part II	Sonnenstein	Part II
Schullwitz	Part II	Seiffersbach	Part I	Soppen	Part II
Schützenhof	Part II	Seifhennersdorf	Part II	Sora	Part II
Schützenwiese	Part I	Seilitz	Part II	Sorga	Part I
Schwaben	Part II	Seitendorf	Part II	Sorga bei Auerbach	Part I
Schwand	Part I	Seitenhain	Part I, II	Sorga bei Reusa	Part I
Schwanneweitz	Part I	Seitgendorf	Part II	Sorgau	Part II
Schwarzbach	Part I	Seitnitz	Part II	Sorg bei Adorf	Part I
Schwarzenberg	Part I	Seligstadt	Part II	Sorge	Part I, II
Schwarzenbrunn	Part I	Sella	Part II	Sorge bei Bärendorf	Part I
Schwarzenreuth	Part I	Selle	Part II	Sorge bei Riechenbach	Part I
Schwarzhammermühle	Part I	Sellerhausen	Part I	Sorge bei Wildenfels	Part I
Schwarzmühle	Part II	Semichau	Part II	Sorgenfrei	Part II
Schwarznauslitz	Part II	Semmelsberg	Part II	Sorgenmühle	Part II
Schwarzreuth	Part I	Senfenhammer	Part II	Soritz	Part II
Schwarzroda	Part I	Serka	Part I	Sörmitz	Part I
Schwarzt Reuthhäuser	Part I	Serkowitz	Part II	Sörnewitz	Part I, II
Schwarzwasser	Part II	Sermitz	Part I	Sornitz	Part II
Schwedei	Part II	Sernewitz	Part II	Sornssig	Part II
Schwednitz	Part I	Seupahn	Part I	Sornzig	Part I
Schwefelhüttenhammer	Part I	Seuritz	Part II	Sörnzig	Part I
Schweikershain	Part I	Seusslitz	Part II	Sosa	Part I, II
Schweinerden	Part II	Siebenbrunn	Part I	Spansberg	Part II
Schweinfurth	Part II	Siebeneichen	Part II	Spansdorf	Part I
Schweinsburg	Part I	Siebenhitz bei Leubnitz	Part I	Spechtritz	Part II
Schweinsdorf	Part II	Siebenhitz bei Magwitz	Part I	Spechtshausen	Part II
Schwepnitz	Part II	Siebenhitz bei Neustadt	Part I	Spernsdorf	Part I
Schweppnitz	Part II	Siebenhitz bei Schönau	Part I	Spittel bei Kamenz	Part II
Schweta bei Döbeln	Part I	Siebenhöfen	Part II	Spittel bei Weissenberg	Part II
Schweta bei Oschatz	Part I	Siebenlehn	Part II	Spittewitz	Part II
Schwettei	Part II	Siebitz bei Göda	Part II	Spittwitz	Part II
Schwochau	Part II	Siebitz bei Marienstern	Part II	Spitzenburg	Part II
Schwoosdorf	Part II	Siedewitzmühle	Part I	Spitzgrund	Part II
Sdier	Part II	Siegfried	Part I	Spitzkunnersdorf	Part II
		Sieglitz bei Klappendorf	Part II	Spitzleithe	Part I

411

KINGDOM OF SAXONY
Parts I and II - Master Index

LOCALITY	PART	LOCALITY	PART	LOCALITY	PART
Spitzmühle	Part I	Stockmühle	Part I	Tannenmühle	Part II
Sporbitz	Part II	Stöfitz	Part I	Tannewitz	Part I
Spreedorf	Part II	Stöhna	Part I	Tannhäuser	Part I
Spreiselmühle bei Gettengrün	Part I	Stollberg	Part II	Tannhof	Part I
Spreiselmühle bei Mühlhausen	Part I	Stollsdorf	Part I	Tännigt	Part I
Spremberg	Part II	Stolpen	Part I, II	Tanzberg	Part I
Spytków	Part II	Stölpgen	Part II	Tanzermühle	Part I
Stacha	Part II	Stolzdorf	Part I	Taschendorf	Part II
Stahlberg	Part II	Stolzenhain	Part II	Taubenheim	Part II
Stahmeln	Part I	Stönzsch	Part I	Taucha	Part I
Stahna	Part II	Storcha	Part II	Tauchnitzmühle	Part I
Stangendorf	Part II	Storchnest	Part II	Taura	Part I
Stangengrün	Part I	Storlwald	Part I	Tauscha	Part I, II
Starrbach	Part II	Störmthal	Part I	Tauschermühle	Part I, II
Staucha	Part II	Stötteritz	Part I	Tauschwitz	Part I
Stauchitz	Part I	Strand	Part II	Tautendorf	Part I
Stauda	Part II	Strassberg	Part I	Tautenhain	Part I
Staudnitz	Part I	Strassenhäuser	Part I	Tautewalde	Part II
Stegvorwerk	Part II	Strassenhäuser am Thonberg	Part I	Technitz	Part I
Stein	Part I	Strassenhäuser		Techritz	Part II
Steina	Part I	bei Volmarsdorf	Part I	Teicha	Part II
Steinbach bei Annaberg	Part II	Strassgräbchen	Part II	Teichhaus	Part I
Steinbach bei Kesselsdorf	Part II	Strauch	Part II	Teichhäuser	Part II
Steinbach bei Lausigk	Part I	Streckewalde	Part II	Teichmühle	Part I, II
Steinbach bei Mohorn	Part II	Strehla	Part I, II	Teichnitz	Part II
Steinbach bei Moritzburg	Part II	Strehlen	Part II	Teichvorwerk	Part II
Steinbachmühle	Part II	Streitfeld	Part II	Tellerhäuser am Kaff	Part II
Steinberg	Part II	Streithaus	Part I	Tellschütz	Part I
Steinborn	Part II	Streitwald	Part I	Temmritz	Part II
Steindöbra	Part I	Streuben	Part I	Tempel	Part II
Steindörfel	Part II	Streuberg	Part I	Tempel bei Frankenhausen	Part I
Steinheidel	Part I	Streumen	Part II	Tempel bei Leitelshain	Part I
Steinhof	Part I	Striegnitz	Part I, II	Temritz	Part II
Steinhof zum		Striesa	Part I	Tennera	Part I
schwarzen Kreuz	Part I	Striesen	Part II	Terpitz	Part I
Steinhof zum weissen Kreuz	Part I	Strocken	Part I	Terpitzsch	Part I
Steinigt	Part I	Strödelmühle	Part I	Terptitz	Part I
Steinigtwolmsdorf	Part II	Stroga	Part II	Tettau	Part II
Stein in Chemnitztal	Part I	Strohschütz	Part II	Thalgut	Part I
Steinmühle	Part I	Stroischen	Part II	Thalheim	Part I, II
Steinpöhl	Part I	Strölla	Part I	Thallwitz	Part I
Steins	Part I	Struppen	Part II	Thammenhain	Part I
Steinsdorf	Part I	Strzegomice	Part II	Thandorf	Part II
Steinwegsmühle	Part I	Stummenmühle	Part I	Thanhof	Part I
Steiten	Part I	Stünz	Part I	Tharandt	Part II
Stelzen	Part I	Stürza	Part II	Thecka	Part I
Stelzendorf	Part II	Stützengrün	Part I	Theckau	Part I
Stelzner Gasthof	Part I	Süppe	Part II	Theeschütz	Part I
Stendten	Part I	Suppo	Part II	Theisewitz	Part II
Stenn	Part I	Sürsen	Part II	Thersdorf	Part I
Stennschütz	Part I	Sützebach	Part I	Theuma	Part I
Stenz	Part II	Sützenbach	Part II	Theusdorf	Part I
Stenzsch	Part I	Syhra	Part I	Thiemendorf	Part II
Sternmühle	Part II	Syrau	Part I	Thiendorf	Part II
Stetzsch	Part II			Thierbach bei Borna	Part I
Steudten	Part II	**T**		Thierbach bei Mühltruff	Part I
Steuermühle	Part I			Thierbach bei Penig	Part I
Steyermühle	Part II	Talpenberg	Part II	Thierbachmühle	Part I
Stiebitz	Part II	Taltitz	Part I	Thierbaum	Part I
Stiesen	Part II	Tammlermühle	Part I	Thierfeld	Part I
Stillerode	Part II	Tanbenpreskeln	Part I	Thiergarten	Part I, II
Stöcken	Part I	Tannaberg	Part II	Thiergarten	Part I
Stockhaus	Part I	Tanndorf	Part I	Thonberg	Part I
Stockhausen	Part I	Tanneberg	Part I, II	Thonhausen (Sachsen portion)	Part I
Stockheim	Part I	Tannenberg	Part II	Thossen	Part I
Stöckigt bei Gutenfürst	Part I	Tannenbergsthal	Part I	Thossfell	Part I
Stöckigt bei Oberlosa	Part I	Tannenhaus	Part I	Thräna	Part I
				Thronitz	Part II

KINGDOM OF SAXONY
Parts I and II - Master Index

LOCALITY	PART	LOCALITY	PART	LOCALITY	PART
Thum	Part II	**U**		**V**	
Thumirnicht	Part I	Uebelessen	Part I	Veitenhäuser	Part I
Thumitz	Part II	Uebigau	Part II	Veitshäuser	Part I
Thümlitz	Part I	Uhlmannsdorf	Part II	Venusberg	Part II
Thurm	Part II	Uhlsdorf	Part I	Vielau	Part I
Thürmsdorf	Part II	Uhyst am Taucher	Part II	Vogelgesang	Part II
Thürnhof	Part I	Uibigau	Part II	Vogelsgrün	Part I
Tiefegrund	Part I	Ulberndorf	Part II	Voigtlaide	Part II
Tiefenau	Part II	Ulbersdorf	Part II	Voigtsberg	Part I
Tiefenbrunn	Part I	Ullendorf	Part II	Voigtsdorf	Part II
Tiefendorf	Part II	Ullersdorf	Part II	Voigtsgrün	Part I
Tirbel	Part I	Ullitz (Sachsen section)	Part I	Voigtshain	Part I
Tirpersdorf	Part I	Ullrichsberg	Part I	Voldern	Part II
Tirschendorf	Part I	Ullrichsmühle	Part I	Volkersdorf	Part II
Tirschheim	Part II	Ulrichsmühle	Part I	Volkmarsdorf	Part I
Tobertitz	Part I	Unckersdorf	Part II	Vorbrücke	Part II
Tolkewitz	Part II	Ungewitz	Part I	Vordercoffebaude	Part II
Töllschütz	Part I	Unsewitz	Part II	Vordergrünbach	Part I
Töpeln	Part I	Unterbergen	Part I	Vorderneudörfel	Part I
Topfseifersdorf	Part I	Unterblauenthal	Part I	Vorderpleuerleite	Part I
Torna	Part I, II	Unterböhlen	Part I	Vorhäuser	Part I
Trachau	Part II	Unterchristgrün	Part I	Vorholz	Part I
Trachenau	Part I	untere Mühle	Part I		
Trachenberge	Part II	Untergöltzsch	Part I	**W**	
Trado	Part II	Unterheinsdorf	Part I		
Tradow	Part II	Unterhermsgrün	Part I	Wachau	Part I, II
Trages	Part I	Unterkemnitzmühle	Part I	Wachelwitz	Part I
Tragis	Part I	Unterklingenthal	Part I	Wachtnitz	Part II
Tragnitz	Part I	Unterlauterbach	Part I	Wachwitz	Part II
Trattlau	Part II	Unterlimbach	Part I	Wadewitz	Part I
Trauschwitz	Part II	Unterlosa	Part I	Waditz	Part II
Trautschen	Part I	Unterlöwenhain	Part II	Wagelwitz	Part I
Trautzschen	Part I	Untermarzgrün	Part I	Wagenbach	Part II
Trebelshain	Part I	Untermühle	Part I, II	Wahlen	Part I
Treben	Part I, II	Unterneumark	Part I	Wahnitz	Part II
Trebigau	Part II	Unterneundorf	Part I	Wahnsdorf	Part II
Trebishain	Part I	Unternitzschka	Part I	Wahren	Part I
Trebnitz	Part I, II	Unterpfannenstiel	Part I	Waitzengrün	Part I
Trebnitzmühle	Part II	Unterpirk	Part I	Waizdorf	Part II
Trebsen	Part I	Unterrauschenthal	Part I	Wald	Part II
Tremnitz	Part I	Unterreichenau	Part I	Walda	Part II
Treppendorf	Part I	UnterReussen	Part I	Walddorf	Part II
Treptitz	Part I	Unterrittersgrün	Part I	Walddörfchen	Part II
Treuen	Part I	Unterrodersdorf	Part I	Waldenburg	Part II
Treugeböhla	Part II	Untersachsenberg	Part I	Wäldgen	Part I
Trieb and der Elster	Part I	Untersachsenfeld	Part I	Waldgrüm	Part I
Trieb bei Bergen	Part I	Unterscheibe	Part I	Waldgut Obertriebel	Part I
Triebischhäuser	Part II	Untersteinpleis	Part I	Waldhaus	Part I
Trifthäuser	Part I	Unterstützengrün	Part I	Waldhaus am Friedrichskiel	Part I
Tröbigau	Part II	Unterthalheim	Part I	Waldhaus am Ortbach	Part I
Trogen	Part I, II	Untertriebel	Part I	Waldhaus am Sonneberg	Part I
Trohnitz	Part I	Untertriebelbach	Part I	Waldhäuser	Part I
Troischau	Part I	Unterweischlitz	Part I	Waldhäuser am Ochsenkopf	Part I
Tronitz	Part I, II	Unterweissig	Part II	Waldhäuser	
Troschenreuth	Part I	Unterwieden	Part I	am vordern Radenberg	Part I
Trossenburg	Part I	Unterwiesenthal	Part II	Waldhäuser bei Seelingstädt	Part I
Trünzig	Part I	Unterwirschnitz	Part I	Waldhäuser bei Trünzig	Part I
Truppen	Part II	Unterwürschnitz	Part I	Waldheim	Part I
Trützschler	Part II	Unterzehren	Part II	Walditz	Part I
Trzciniec	Part II	Unterzwota	Part I	Waldkirchen	Part I, II
Tscharnitz	Part II	Unwürde	Part II	Waldmühle	Part I
Tschaschwitz	Part II	Ursprung	Part II	Waldpfütze	Part I
Tschorna bei Lauske	Part II	Uttewalde	Part II	Waldsachsen	Part I
Tschornau bei Kamenz	Part II			Waldschenke	Part II
Türbel	Part I			Waldschenke bei Marienthal	Part I
Türchau	Part II			Wallbach	Part I
Turoszów	Part II			Wallengrün	Part I
Tuttendorf	Part II				

KINGDOM OF SAXONY
Parts I and II - Master Index

LOCALITY	PART	LOCALITY	PART	LOCALITY	PART
Wallroda	Part II	Weissig am Raschütz	Part II	Wiesa	Part II
Waltersdorf	Part II	Weissig bei Bautzen	Part II	Wiesenbad	Part I, II
Walthersdorf	Part II	Weissig bei Biehla	Part II	Wiesenburg	Part I
Walzig	Part I	Weissig bei Kamenz	Part II	Wiesengrund	Part I
Wanne	Part I	Weissig bei Königstein	Part II	Wiesenhaus	Part I
Wanscha	Part II	Weissig bei Skassa	Part II	Wiesenmühle	Part I, II
Wantewitz	Part II	Weissnauslitz	Part II	Wiesenthal	Part I, II
Wartha	Part II	Weisstropp	Part II	Wietrau	Part II
Waschleiteh	Part I	Weiters Glashütte	Part I	Wigancice Żytawskie	Part II
Waschleithen	Part I	Weiterswiese	Part I	Wildbach	Part I
Waschleute	Part I	Weitzschen	Part II	Wildberg	Part I, II
Wasewitz	Part I	Weitzschenhain	Part I	Wildenau	Part I
Wasserburg	Part II	Weixdorf	Part II	Wildenburg	Part II
Wassergrund	Part II	Welka bei Pulssnitz	Part II	Wildenfels	Part I
Wasserkretscham	Part II	Welkau	Part II	Wildenhain	Part I, II
Wasserloh	Part I	Wellerswalde	Part I	Wildenthal	Part I
Watzschwitz	Part I	Wellixande	Part II	Wilderberg	Part I
Wauden	Part II	Welschhufe	Part II	Wildhaus	Part II
Wawitz	Part II	Welxande	Part II	Wilhelminenberg	Part I
Wechselburg	Part I	Wendischbaselitz	Part II	Wilhelmsheide	Part I
Wechselmühle	Part I	Wendischbora	Part II	Wilischmühle	Part I
Wednig	Part I	Wendischcunnersdorf	Part II	Wilischthal	Part II
Weesenstein	Part II	Wendischenbohra	Part II	Wilkau	Part I
Wegefarth	Part II	Wendischkarsdorf	Part II	Wilmsdorf	Part II
Wehlen	Part II	Wendisch Luppa	Part I	Wilsch	Part II
Wehlstädtel	Part II	Wendischpaulsdorf	Part II	Wilschdorf	Part II
Wehrda	Part I	Wendischrottmannsdorf	Part I	Wilschmühle	Part I
Wehrsdorf	Part II	Wendischsohland	Part II	Wilschwitz	Part II
Weicha	Part II	Wendishain	Part I	Wilsdruf	Part II
Weicholdswälder Vorwerke	Part II	Wenigborna	Part I	Wilsdruff	Part II
Weichteritz	Part I	Wenigenborn	Part I	Wilthen	Part II
Weickersdorf	Part II	Wenigossa	Part I	Wilzschhaus	Part I
Weida	Part II	Wenzelhaus	Part I	Wind	Part II
Weide	Part II	Werda	Part I	Windmühlenhaus	Part I
Weidenhof	Part I	Werdau	Part I	Windorf	Part I, II
Weidensdorf	Part II	Wermsdorf	Part I	Windschenke	Part II
Weiderode	Part I	Wernesgrün	Part I	Wingendorf	Part II
Weidigt bei Adorf	Part I	Wernitzgrün	Part I	Winkelmühle	Part I
Weidigt bei Bobenneukirchen	Part I	Wernsdorf bei Glauchau	Part II	Winkeln	Part I
Weiditz	Part I	Wernsdorf bei Lauterstein	Part I	Winkwitz	Part II
Weidlichshäuser	Part I	Wernsdorf bei Penig	Part I	Winn	Part I
Weidlitz	Part II	Wernsgrün	Part I	Winnknock	Part I
Weigmannsdorf	Part II	Wesenstein	Part II	Winselburg	Part I
Weigsdorf im Gebirge	Part II	Wesnitz	Part II	Winterscheuke	Part I
Weikersdorf	Part II	Wessel	Part II	Wipplas	Part I
Weinböhla	Part II	Wessnitzmühle	Part II	Wittchendorf	Part I
Weindischfehra	Part II	Westewitz	Part I	Wittgendorf	Part II
Weinleite	Part I	Wetitz	Part I	Wittgensdorf	Part I
Weinleithenhaus	Part I	Wetro	Part II	Wittichsthal	Part I
Weinsdorf	Part I	Wetterhütte	Part I	Witzmühle	Part I
Weintraube	Part I	Wetteritz	Part I	Witznitz	Part I
Weinwiese	Part II	Wettersdorf	Part II	Witzschdorf	Part II
Weisa	Part II	Wetterwitz	Part II	Witzschendorf	Part II
Weischlitz	Part I	Wetzelsgrün	Part I	Wohla bei Löbau	Part II
Weisenborn	Part I, II	Wetzelsmühle	Part I	Wohla bei Pulssnitz	Part II
Weisensand	Part I	Wetzlarsgrün	Part I	Wohlbach	Part I
Weisenstein	Part I	Wichstanda	Part II	Wohlhausen	Part I
Weissbach bei Königsbrück	Part II	Wickersdorf	Part II	Wolfersgrün	Part I
Weissbach bei Königsfeld	Part I	Wickershain	Part I	Wölfnitz	Part II
Weissbach bei Pulssnitz	Part II	Wiedenberg	Part I	Wolfsberg	Part I
Weissbach bei Schneeberg	Part I	Wiedenleithe	Part I	Wolfsberg bei Neusorge	Part II
Weissbach bei Zschopau	Part II	Wiederau	Part I	Wolfschmiede	Part II
Weissenberg	Part II	Wiederberg	Part I	Wolfsgrün	Part I, II
Weissenborn	Part I, II	Wiederoda	Part I	Wolfsgrund	Part II
Weissenbrunn	Part I	Wiedersberg	Part I	Wolfshain	Part I
Weissenstein	Part I	Wiednitzer	Part II	Wolfsmühle	Part I
Weissig	Part II	Wiehra	Part I	Wolfspfütze	Part I

414

KINGDOM OF SAXONY
Parts I and II - Master Index

LOCALITY	PART	LOCALITY	PART	LOCALITY	PART
Wolfsstande	Part I	Zehren	Part II	Zöllsdorf	Part I
Wolfsthal	Part I	Zeicha	Part I	Zollwitz	Part I
Wolftitz	Part I	Zeichen	Part II	Zöpen	Part I
Wolka	Part II	Zeidelweide	Part I	Zöschau	Part I
Wölka	Part II	Zeiffignest	Part I	Zöthain	Part II
Wolkau	Part II	Zeifiggesang	Part I	Zottewitz	Part II
Wölkau	Part II	Zeisholz	Part II	Zschaachwitz	Part I
Wolkenburg	Part I	Zeissholz	Part II	Zschaagwitz	Part I
Wolkenstein	Part II	Zeithain	Part II	Zschackwitz	Part I
Wölkisch	Part II	Zeititz	Part I	Zschäckwitz	Part II
Wölknitz	Part II	Zella	Part I	Zschadratz	Part I
Wollsdorf	Part I	Zellersmühle	Part I	Zschagast	Part I
Wöllsdorf	Part I	Zellmen	Part II	Zschaiten	Part II
Wolsdorf	Part I	Zennewitz	Part I	Zschaitz	Part I
Worbs	Part II	Zerna	Part II	Zschanitz	Part I, II
Worderreissig	Part I	Zescha	Part II	Zschannewitz	Part I
Wuhnitz	Part II	Zeschnig	Part II	Zschärtnitz	Part II
Wuhsen	Part II	Zeschwitz	Part I	Zschaschwitz	Part II
Wuischke bei Gröditz	Part II	Zetha	Part I	Zscheckwitz	Part II
Wuischke bei Hochkirch	Part II	Zethau	Part II	Zscheila	Part II
Wuischker Mühle	Part II	Zetta	Part II	Zscheilitz	Part II
Wülknitz	Part II	Zettelhaus	Part II	Zscheisewitz	Part II
Wünschendorf	Part II	Zettelsgrün	Part I	Zschepa	Part II
Wunschwitz	Part II	Zetteritz	Part I	Zschepplitz	Part I
Wurbis	Part II	Zettlarsgrün	Part I	Zschertnitz	Part II
Wurgwitz	Part II	Zettlitz	Part I	Zschetzsch	Part I
Wurschen	Part II	Zetzsch	Part II	Zschickenmühle	Part I
Würschnitz	Part II	Zeuckritz	Part I	Zschiedge	Part II
Würschütz	Part I	Zeughäuser	Part I	Zschieren	Part II
Würschwitz	Part I	Zeunitz	Part I	Zschieschen	Part II
Wurzen	Part I	Ziegelgrund	Part I, II	Zschillchau	Part II
Wüstanda	Part II	Ziegelguth	Part I	Zschillen	Part I
Wüstenbrand	Part II	Ziegelheim	Part II	Zschillichau	Part II
Wüstenhain	Part I	Ziegelhütten	Part I	Zschirla	Part I
Wüstenschlette	Part II	Ziegelschenne	Part II	Zschiskenmühle	Part I
Wüsteschlette	Part II	Ziegeluhlsdorf	Part II	Zschochau	Part II
Wüsthetzdorf	Part II	Ziegenfoor	Part I	Zschockau	Part I
Wüstungstein	Part I	Ziegengeför	Part I	Zschocken	Part I
Wyhra	Part I	Ziegenhain	Part II	Zschöllau	Part I
Wyszków	Part II	Zieglerthal	Part II	Zschopau	Part II
		Ziegra	Part I	Zschöpchen	Part I
Z		Ziemberg	Part I	Zschopenthal	Part II
		Zieschen	Part II	Zschoppach	Part I
Zaaschwitz	Part I	Zieschütz	Part II	Zschoppeshain	Part I
Zabeltitz	Part II	Ziessen	Part I	Zschöppichen	Part I
Zachariashaus	Part I	Zietsch	Part II	Zschorlau	Part I
Zadel	Part II	Zimmersacher	Part I	Zschorna	Part II
Zadera	Part I	Zinnberg	Part I	Zschorna bei Murzen	Part I
Zahnmühle	Part I	Zinnwald	Part II	Zschorna bei Radeburg	Part II
Zaschendorf	Part II	Zischkowitz	Part II	Zschornau	Part II
Zaschwitz	Part I	Zissen	Part I	Zschornmühle	Part II
Zassnitz	Part I	Zittau	Part I	Zuckelhausen	Part I
Zasuchwitz	Part I	Zittel	Part II	Zuckmantel	Part II
Zatonie	Part II	Zitzschewig	Part II	zum Steiger	Part II
Zatzschke	Part II	Zobes	Part I	Zuschendorf	Part II
Zaukerode	Part II	Zöbigker	Part I	Zweenfurth	Part I
Zaulsdorf	Part I	Zöbisch	Part I	Zweinaundorf	Part I
Zaunhaus	Part II	Zöbischhäuser	Part I	Zweinig	Part I
Zausswitz	Part I	Zoblitz	Part II	Zwenkau	Part I
Zävertitz	Part I	Zöblitz	Part II	Zwickau	Part I
Zeche	Part I	Zochau	Part II	Zwierzschen	Part I
Zechenbach	Part I	Zockau	Part II	Zwiesel	Part II
Zedlitz	Part I	Zöhda	Part I	Zwirzschka	Part II
Zehda	Part I	Zoitzmühle	Part I	Zwochau	Part I
Zehista	Part II	Zollhaus Berghäusel	Part II	Zwokenthal	Part I
Zehmen	Part I	Zöllmen	Part II	Zwönitz	Part II
Zehmen'sches Gut	Part II	Zöllnitz	Part I	Zwoschwitz	Part I
Zehndner Häuser	Part I	Zollschwitz	Part I	Zwota	Part I